A Laboratory Course for

Programming

with

Java™

Nell Dale

University of Texas, Austin

JONES AND BARTLETT PUBLISHERS

Sudbury, Massachusetts

BOSTON   TORONTO   LONDON   SINGAPORE

P9-DDF-163

World Headquarters
Jones and Bartlett Publishers
40 Tall Pine Drive
Sudbury, MA 01776
978-443-5000
info@jbpub.com
www.jbpub.com

Jones and Bartlett Publishers
Canada
2406 Nikanna Road
Mississauga, ON L5C 2W6
CANADA

Jones and Bartlett Publishers
International
Barb House, Barb Mews
London W6 7PA
UK

ISBN 0-7637-2463-7

Library of Congress Cataloging-in-Publication Data not available at time of printing.

Editor-in-Chief, College: J. Michael Stranz
Production Manager: Amy Rose
Associate Editor: Theresa DiDonato
Associate Production Editor: Karen C. Ferreira
Production Assistant: Jenny McIsaac
Senior Marketing Manager: Nathan Schultz
Composition: AnnMarie Lemoine
Cover Design: Kristin E. Ohlin
Manufacturing Buyer: Therese Bräuer
Printing and Binding: Courier Stoughton
Cover Printing: Courier Stoughton

Printed in the United States of America
07 06 05 04 03   10 9 8 7 6 5 4 3 2

Need for Support in Learning Java

For about 20 years, the introductory computer science course was taught mostly in Pascal. About ten years ago there was a move toward C++ in place of Pascal, followed almost immediately by a move towards Java. Even the strongest advocates for these changes realize that C++ and Java are more difficult than Pascal for most beginning students to learn.

C++ and Java were not designed with the beginning student in mind. Rather, they were designed for commercial programming environments. Professional programmers are assumed to know what they mean and mean what they say. Beginning students, on the other hand, often do not know what they mean and even more often do not mean what they say. Hence, it is essential that students understand the syntax and semantics of each construct as they go along. Closed laboratory activities seem an ideal way to make this happen.

Closed Laboratories in Computer Science

The Denning Report[1] introduced the term *closed laboratories* without defining exactly what they were. At least four different definitions subsequently surfaced.

1. A scheduled time when students work on their programming assignments under supervision.
2. A scheduled drill-and-practice time when students work on mini-problems under supervision.
3. The use of specially prepared laboratory materials where students interact with the computer as they would a microscope or Bunsen burner. The labs should help the student discover principles and solutions under supervision. This definition is closest to the spirit of the Denning Report.
4. A combination of two or more of the above.

[1] Denning, P. J. (chair) "Computing as a Discipline" *Communications of the ACM*, Vol. 32, No. 1, pp. 9-23.

With the publication of the Curriculum '91[2] report, laboratory exercises were suggested for many of the knowledge units. However, a precise definition of what constituted a closed laboratory activity was not included. And, in fact, many of the activities suggested could be done equally well in a non-supervised (or open) setting.

Laboratory activities as defined in this manual are a combination of definitions 2 and 3.

Open versus Closed Laboratories

Although the Denning Report and Curriculum '91 imply that laboratory exercises should be done under supervision, we do not feel that this is essential. Our view is that closed laboratory exercises are valuable for two reasons: the exercises themselves and the extra contact time with a faculty member or a teaching assistant. If a closed laboratory environment is not an option, the students can still benefit from working the exercises on their own.

Organization of the Manual

Each chapter contains three types of activities: Prelab, Inlab, and Postlab. The Prelab activities include a reading review assignment and simple paper and pencil exercises. The Inlab activities are broken into lessons, each of which represents a concept covered in the chapter. Each lesson is broken into exercises that thoroughly demonstrate the concept. The Postlab exercises are a collection of outside programming assignments appropriate for each chapter. Each exercise requires that the students apply the concepts covered in the chapter.

When this manual is being used in a closed-laboratory setting, we suggest that the Prelab activities be done before the students come to lab. The students can spend the first few minutes of the laboratory checking their answers (Lesson 1 for each chapter). The Inlab activities are designed to take approximately two hours, the usual time for a closed laboratory. However, an instructor can tailor the chapter to the level of the class by assigning only a partial set of exercises or by shortening the time allowed.

The Postlab activities present a selection of programming projects. We do not suggest that all of them be assigned. In most cases, one should be sufficient, unless there are several related problems.

If the manual is not being used in a closed-laboratory setting, an instructor can assign all or a selection of the Inlab activities to be done independently (see the section "Flexibility" below). In either a closed or open setting, many of the Inlab and Postlab activities can be done in groups.

Theoretical Basis for the Activities

The decision to break each chapter into three types of activities is based on the work of Benjamin Bloom, who developed a taxonomy of six increasingly difficult levels of achievement in the cognitive domain.[3] In developing the activities for this manual, we

---

[2] Tucker, A. B. (Ed.) "Computing Curricula 1991: Report of the ACM/IEEE-CS Joint Curriculum Task Force. Final Draft, December 17. ACM Order Number 201910. IEEE Computer Society Press Order Number 2220.

[3] Bloom, Benjamin *Taxonomy of Educational Objectives: Handbook I: Cognitive Domain*. New York: David McKay, 1956.

combined Bloom's six categories into three. These categories are defined below in terms of the concrete example of learning an algorithm (or language-related construct).

Recognition   The student can trace the algorithm and determine what the output should be for a given data set (no transfer).

Generation   The student can generate a very similar algorithm (near transfer).

Projection   The student can modify the algorithm to accomplish a major change (far transfer), can apply the algorithm in a different context, can combine related algorithms, and can compare algorithms.

The Prelab activities are at the recognition level. Most of the Inlab activities are at the generation level with a few projection-level activities included where appropriate. The Postlab activities are projection-level activities.

The activities are also influenced by the work of Kolb and others on how students learn.[4] The more actively involved students are in the learning process, the more they learn. Reading and writing are forms of active involvement. Therefore, the Prelab activities begin with a reading review, and many of the exercises ask the students to write explanations of what happened. Just watching a program run and looking at the answer is a passive activity, but having to write the answer transforms the exercise into an active one.

Flexibility

A Laboratory Course for Programming with Java is designed to allow the instructor maximum flexibility. Each chapter has an assignment cover sheet that provides a checklist in tabular form. The first column of the table in the Assignment Cover Sheet lists the chapter activities, in the second column students can check which activities have been assigned, in the third column they can record what output is to be turned in, and the fourth column is for the instructor to use for grading. The pages are perforated so students can easily tear out sheets to turn in.

Student Resource Disk for Java

The Web site contains the classes, class shells (partial programs), and data files. A copy of most of the classes or class shells is listed before the exercises that use them. Programs used for debugging exercises are not shown, however. Because some of the exercises ask the student to go back to the original version of a previous class or class shell, we suggest that the student copy the files and work from the copy.

The files are divided into subdirectories, one for each chapter. The classes and class shells are stored in files under the class name with a `.java` extension. Packages are stored in a directory bearing the package name. Compilation units within a package are stored under the name of the public class with a `.java` extension. The Web site that contains these files is http://computerscience.jbpub.com/ppsjava

Acknowledgments

No author writes in a vacuum. There is always formal and informal feedback from colleagues. Thanks to those of you in my department who patiently answered "by the way" questions about Java. Thanks to Chip Weems at UMass Amherst who taught me

---

[4] Svinicki, Marilla D., and Dixon Nancy M. "The Kolb Model Modified for Classroom Activities" *College Teaching*, Vol. 35, No. 4, Fall, pp. 141-146.

Java. Thanks also to those who reviewed *Java and Software Design* and added so much to my knowledge and appreciation of the language: John Connely, John Beidler, Hang Lau, Thomas Mertz, Bina Ramamurthy, James Roberts, David Shultz, Kenneth Slonneger, and Sylvia Sorkin. Thanks also to the reviewers of *Programming and Problem Solving with Java* whose insightful comments were much appreciated: Rama Chakrapani, Tennessee Technological University; Ilyas Cicekli, University of Central Florida; Jose Cordova, University of Louisiana at Monroe; Mike Litman, Western Illinois University; Rathika Rajaravivarma, Central Connecticut State University. A special thanks goes to Dale Skrien at Colby College who reviewed the first edition of this manuscript on a very tight schedule and gave many helpful suggestions.

Thanks to AnnMarie Lemoine along with the many people at Jones and Bartlett who contributed so much, especially J. Michael Stranz, Anne Spencer, Jenny McIsaac, Theresa DiDonato, and Amy Rose.

N.D.

Overview of Programming and Problem Solving

- ■ To be able to log on to a computer.
- ■ To be able to do the following tasks on a computer.

  - Change the active (work) directory.

  - List the files in a directory.

- ■ To be able to do the following tasks using an editor and a Java compiler.

  - Load a file containing a program.

  - Alter a file containing a program.

  - Save a file.

  - Print a file.

  - Compile a program.

  - Run a program.

  - Change a program and rerun it.

  - Correct a program with errors.

  - Enter and run a program.

  - Exit the system.

Laboratory 1: Assignment Cover Sheet

Name _____ Date _____

Section _____

Fill in the following table showing which exercises have been assigned for each lesson and check what you are to submit: (1) lab sheets, (2) listings of output files, and/or (3) listings of code. Your instructor or teaching assistant (TA) can use the Completed column for grading purposes.

Activities	Assigned: Check or list exercise numbers	Submit (1) (2) (3)			Completed
Prelab					
Review					
Prelab Assignment					
Inlab					
Lesson 1-1: Check Prelab Exercises					
Lesson 1-2: Basic File Operations					
Lesson 1-3: Compiling and Running a Program					
Lesson 1-4: Editing, Running, and Printing a Program File					
Lesson 1-5: Running a Program with an Error					
Lesson 1-6: Entering, Compiling, and Running a New Program					
Postlab					

Prelab Activities

Review

A computer is a programmable electronic device that can store, retrieve, and process data. The verbs store, retrieve, and process relate to the five basic physical components of the computer: the memory unit, the arithmetic/logic unit, the control unit, input devices, and output devices. These physical components are called computer hardware. The programs that are available to run on a computer are called software. Writing the programs that make up the software is called programming.

Programming

A program is a sequence of instructions written to perform a specific task. Programming is the process of defining the sequence of instructions. There are two phases in this process: determining the task that needs doing and expressing the solution in a sequence of instructions.

The process of programming always begins with a problem. Programs are not written in isolation; they are written to solve problems. Determining what needs to be done means outlining the solution to the problem. This first phase, then, is the problem-solving phase.

The second phase, expressing the solution in a sequence of instructions, is the implementation phase. Here, the general solution outlined in the problem-solving phase is converted into a specific solution (a program in a specific language). Testing is part of both phases. The general solution must be shown to be correct before it is translated into a program.

Let's demonstrate the process with the following problem.

Problem: Calculate the average rainfall over a period of days.

Discussion: To do the job by hand, you would write down the number of inches of rain that had fallen each day. Then you would add the figures up and divide the total by the number of days. This is exactly the algorithm we use in the program.

Algorithm: (on the next page)

Average Rainfall

> Get total inches of rain
> if number of days is zero then
>   Average cannot be computed
> else
>   Set average to total / number of days

The first line in this algorithm box contains the name of a *subprogram*. The subprogram (or subalgorithm) is named here as a task without saying how it is to be done. This task is expanded separately in the next algorithm box. The next four lines in this box are a *selection construct*: One thing is done if the number of days is zero; another thing is done if the number of days is not zero.

Get Total Inches of Rain

> while there are more days
>   Get inches
>   Set total to total + inches

This algorithm box represents a *loop construct*: The task of getting the number of inches and adding it to the total is repeated for each day.

The combination of the statements within the loop illustrates the *sequence construct*: The task of getting inches is followed immediately by the task of adding the inches to the total.

The Java program that implements this algorithm is given below. Don't worry if you don't understand it. At this stage, you're not expected to. Before long, you will be able to understand all of it.

Incidentally, the information between the symbols /* and */ is meant for the human reader of the program. This kind of information is called a *comment* and is ignored by the Java compiler. Information from // to the end of a line is also a comment.

```
/* Class RainFall calculates the average rainfall over a
   period of days.  The number of days and the rain statistics
   are in file Rain.in */

import java.io.*;
```

```java
public class RainFall
{
  // Declare dataFile for input
  private static BufferedReader dataFile;

  static double getInches(BufferedReader dataFile,
    int numberDays) throws IOException
  // Reads and returns the total inches of rain
  {
    double total = 0.0;
    double inches;
    int days = 1;
    while (days <= numberDays)
    {
      inches =
        Double.parseDouble(dataFile.readLine());
      total = total + inches;
      days++;
    }
    return total;
  }


  public static void main(String[] args) throws IOException
  // Main is where execution starts.  It opens the data file,
  //   reads the number of days of rain to be totaled, calls an
  //   auxiliary method to read and sum the rainfall, and
  //   prints the average rainfall on the screen
  {
    double totalRain;
    int numDays;
    double average;
    // Instantiate and open the data file
    dataFile = new BufferedReader(
      new FileReader("rainFile.in"));
    // Input the number of days
    numDays = Integer.parseInt(dataFile.readLine());

    totalRain = getInches(dataFile, numDays);

    if (numDays == 0)
      System.out.println("Average cannot be computed "
          + "for 0 days.");
    else
    {
      average = totalRain / numDays;
      System.out.println("The average rainfall over " +
        numDays + " days is " + average);
    }
    dataFile.close();
  }
}
```

This application illustrates subprograms, selection, looping, and sequencing. There is a fifth construct, *asynchronous events*, that is not represented here. If this algorithm asked the user to enter a rainfall amount and press a button, the input would be event driven. This process is an example of asynchronous processing. The program would request a data value from the screen and wait until the user entered the value and pressed a button. The pressing of the button is an asynchronous event.

Getting Started

Certain Java systems provide an integrated environment for the creation and execution of Java programs. For example, Cafe and CodeWarrior, which run on PCs and Macs, provide such an environment. The compiler, the editor, and the runtime system are all bundled together into one system. Other Java compilers come separately so that you must use a general-purpose editor to enter your program. You compile the program and then run it. There are far too many systems for us to describe any of them in detail. Therefore, we use an analogy to describe the process of entering and running your program.

When you first get on a machine (*log in*), the *operating system* is the software that is running. You can think of the operating system as a hallway that connects all the other pieces of software. You enter the name of the software you want to use, and the operating system provides it. When you finish using the software, you must come back to the operating system (the hallway) before you can use another piece of software.

Each piece of software is like a doorway. The operating system opens the door and ushers you into the room where the software you want to use is kept. In the *editor*, you create a file of written information. This file may contain a program or data for a program.

To those of you who have not worked with an editor before, think of it as a program that allows you to use your keyboard and screen like a very smart electronic typewriter. A *file* is the information that you type in through the keyboard. You see what you type on the screen. Commands to the editor do what you would do manually with a typewriter. These allow you to change and rearrange letters, words, and sentences. A file resides in an area in secondary storage, which has a name, and is used to hold a collection of data. The data itself is also referred to as a file.

When you are satisfied with what you've typed, you give your file a name and tell the editor to save it for you. Giving a file a name is like putting information into a folder with a label on it. You can pick up the file and carry it with you from one room to another.

When you leave the editor, the operating system comes back with a prompt that says it's ready for you to tell it where you want to go next. If you've created a Java program, you say that you want to *compile* (translate) your file (go to the Java room). The operating system opens the door, and you hand your file folder to the Java compiler.

The Java compiler attempts to translate your program. If the program contains grammatical errors (errors in syntax), the compiler tells you so. You then have to go back to the editing room to correct the mistakes. When your Java program finally compiles correctly, the Java compiler leaves the object program (the translated code) in a file.

You tell the operating system that you are ready to run the object program. The file containing the translated program is taken into the execute room, where it is run. It's here, in the execute room, that the problem your program was written to solve actually is solved.

When you're finished and ready to quit (*log out*), you tell the operating system. It opens the door marked exit, and you can leave.

Some systems bundle the editing room, the compiling room, and the executing room into one luxurious suite. For example, in CodeWarrior, you say "CodeWarrior IDE." You are then handed a menu of the things that you can do: Create a new file, modify an old file, compile a program, or run a program. You even have the option of asking for help. You make a choice either by using a mouse (a pointing device) or by pressing a function key on the keyboard. Several of these choices then provide you with a second menu from which to choose. Integrated systems are *user-friendly* systems: You are never left stranded; you are always guided through the input (edit), compile, and run cycle by the use of these menus that appear at the top of your screen.

Laboratory 1: Prelab Assignment

Name _____ Date _____

Section _____

Your instructor should provide a handout describing the system that you are using.

Exercise 1: What computer are you using?

Exercise 2: What operating system are you using?

Exercise 3: What Java system are you using?

Exercise 4: Is your Java system an integrated system, or is the editor separate from the compiler?

Exercise 5: If your editor is separate, which editor are you using?

Exercise 6: If you are not using an integrated system, what are the compile, run, and edit commands you are using?

Lesson 1-1: Check Prelab Exercises

Name _____   Date _____

Section _____

Exercise 1: What computer are you using? IBM-compatible PCs, Macintosh computers, and UNIX or Linux workstations are common in this course. You also might be using a terminal to a computer network.

Exercise 2: What operating system are you using? Windows '95, '98, or 2000, Macintosh, and UNIX or Linux are common operating systems.

Exercise 3: What Java system are you using? There are lots of choices, but it must be compatible with the operating system that you are using.

Exercise 4: Is your Java system an integrated system, or is the editor separate from the compiler? You only have two choices here: either it is integrated or it is not.

Exercise 5: If your editor is separate, which editor are you using? Word and WordPerfect are two common editors on PCs. Emacs and vi are two editors for workstations.

Exercise 6: If you are not using an integrated system, what are the compile, run, and edit commands you are using? You have to check with your instructor for this one.

Lesson 1-2: Basic File Operations

Name _____   Date _____

Section _____

Exercise 1: Follow your instructor's instructions on how to log on to the system.

Exercise 2: Regardless of the system you are using, the memory should be divided up into hierarchical subsections called directories. At any one time, you are in a directory. List all the contents of the directory you are in when you log on to the system. (*Hint*: The command to list a directory on PC compatibles is **dir**; on UNIX machines it is **ls**. In a Windows or Macintosh system, you click on the directory name.)

Exercise 3: Is one of the items listed in the directory itself a directory? If so, change into that directory and list its contents.

Exercise 4: Enter the editor. Type your name on the screen and save the file.

Exercise 5: Bring file `RainFall.java` into your editor. Look through it carefully; it contains the Java program shown in the review. Save the file.

Exercise 6: Bring file `Rain2.java` into your editor. Examine it carefully. It is the same as file `rain.java` with the formatting changed and the class name changed. (Which is easier for the human to read?) Save the file.

Lesson 1-3: Compiling and Running a Program

Name _____ Date _____

Section _____

Exercise 1: Compile and run application `RainFall` in file `RainFall.java`. How many inches of rain were there?

Exercise 2: Compile and run application `Rain2` in file `Rain2.java`. How many inches of rain were there?

Exercise 3: Are you surprised that the results were the same in Exercises 1 and 2? What does that tell you about the differences between how the compiler views the text of a program and how the user views the text of a program?

Exercise 4: Compile and run application `WriteName` in file `WriteName.java`. What is printed on the screen?

Lesson 1–4: Editing, Running, and Printing a Program File

Name _____ Date _____

Section _____

Exercise 1: Bring file `WriteName.java` to the screen. Replace the name Nell Dale with your own name. Compile and run the program. What is printed on the screen?

Exercise 2: Did you notice that there is no period after the name and that the line of asterisks is not even? Go back and edit this program so that a period follows the name and the two lines contain the same number of asterisks. Compile and run your program. What is printed on the screen?

Exercise 3: Save your changed file.

Exercise 4: You now need to print out a copy of your changed file from Exercise 3 to turn in to your instructor. Follow your instructor's instructions on how to print a file.

Lesson 1-5: Running a Program with an Error

Name _____   Date _____

Section _____

Exercise 1: Compile application `Error` in file `Error.java`. The error message you get and what happens when this occurs depends on the Java compiler you are using. Describe the error message, and tell what happened.

Exercise 2: Go back into the editor and correct the error. (There is a semicolon missing.) Compile and run your program. What is the output?

Lesson 1-6: Entering, Compiling, and Running a New Program

Name __Jerry Reed_____ Date _____

Section _____

Exercise 1: Enter the editor and key in the following program. You are not expected to understand what it does; just copy it exactly as shown.

```
// Program Multiples calculates the square and cube of a value.
public class Multiples
{
  public static void main(String[] args)
  {
    final int VALUE = 5;
    System.out.println("The number is " + VALUE);
    System.out.println("" + VALUE + " squared  is " +
      VALUE*VALUE);
    System.out.println("" + VALUE + " cubed is " +
      VALUE*VALUE*VALUE);
  }
}
```

Exercise 2: When you have finished keying in this program, try to compile it. If you have made any typing errors, correct them and try to compile the program again.

Exercise 3: When the program compiles without any errors, you are ready to run it. What is written on the screen?

Exercise 4: Change the 5 in line six to 17 and recompile and run the program. What is written on the screen?

Exercise 5: Exit the system.

Postlab Activities

Exercise 1: Key in the following program, compile it, and run it.

```java
// Program Stars prints three rows of asterisks

public class Stars
{
  public static void main(String[] args)
  {
    final String MSG1 = "***********";
    final String MSG2 = " ********* ";
    final String MSG3 = "  *******   ";
    System.out.println(MSG1);
    System.out.println(MSG2);
    System.out.println(MSG3);
  }
}
```

Exercise 2: Edit program `Stars` so that it prints five asterisks centered on the fourth line, three asterisks centered on the fifth line, and one asterisk centered on the sixth line. Compile and run your program.

Exercise 3: Using program `Stars` as a model, write a program that prints the same pattern on the screen but with a dollar sign symbol rather than an asterisk.

Java Syntax and Semantics, Classes and Objects

Objectives

- To be able to compile and run a Java program from disk.

- To be able to modify the various parts of a program and observe what these changes do to the program's output.

- To be able to construct output statements that send information to the output stream.

- To be able to construct an expression made up of characters, strings, and the concatenation operator.

- To be able to construct assignment statements to accomplish a stated task.

- To be able to construct input statements that read strings from the keyboard.

- To be able to debug a program with syntax errors.

- To be able to debug a program with logic errors.

Laboratory 2: Assignment Cover Sheet

Name _____   Date _____

Section _____

Fill in the following table showing which exercises have been assigned for each lesson and check what you are to submit: (1) lab sheets, (2) listings of output files, and/or (3) listings of code. Your instructor or teaching assistant (TA) can use the Completed column for grading purposes.

Activities	Assigned: Check or list exercise numbers	Submit (1) (2) (3)			Completed
Prelab					
Review					
Prelab Assignment					
Inlab					
Lesson 2-1: Check Prelab Exercises					
Lesson 2-2: Components of a Program					
Lesson 2-3: Sending Information to the Output Stream					
Lesson 2-4: Reading Data Interactively					
Lesson 2-5: Debugging					
Postlab					

Prelab Activities

Review

There are two basic parts to a Java program: (1) instructions to the Java compiler and (2) instructions that describe the processing to be done. However, before we can describe these instructions, we must have a way of naming things so that we can tell the compiler about them and describe what we want to have done to them. We name things (classes, data objects, and actions) by giving them an *identifier*. An identifier is made up of letters, numbers, and underscores, but must begin with a letter or an underscore. We use the words *identifier* and *name* interchangeably.

Beware: Java is case sensitive. This means that Value, VALUE, value, and vaLue are four separate identifiers. In fact, we can construct 32 distinct identifiers from these five letters by varying the capitalization.

Java programmers use certain conventions to provide visual cues about what an identifier is naming. Class identifiers begin with an uppercase letter, object and action (method) identifiers begin with a lowercase letter, and constant identifiers are all uppercase.

Program Structure

Let's examine the following Java program. We have numbered the lines so that we can discuss them. Note that programs are often called applications in Java.

```
1.   // Program Rhyme prints out a nursery rhyme
2.   public class Rhyme
3.   {
4.     public static void main(String[] args)
5.     {
6.       final char SEMI_COLON = ';';
7.       final String VERB1 = "went up ";
8.       final String VERB2 = "down came ";
9.       final String VERB3 = "washed ";
10.      final String VERB4 = "out came ";
11.      final String VERB5 = "dried up ";

12.      String firstLine;
13.      String secondLine;
14.      String thirdLine;
15.      String fourthLine;

16.      firstLine = "The itsy bitsy spider " + VERB1 +
           "the water spout";
17.      secondLine = VERB2 + "the rain and " + VERB3 +
           "the spider out";
18.      thirdLine = VERB4 + "the sun and " + VERB5 +
           "all the rain";
19.      fourthLine = "and the itsy bitsy spider " + VERB1 +
           "the spout again";

20.      System.out.println(firstLine + SEMI_COLON);
21.      System.out.println(secondLine + SEMI_COLON);
```

```
22.     System.out.print(thirdLine + SEMI_COLON);
23.     System.out.println();
24.     System.out.println(fourthLine + '.');
25.   }
26. }
```

Line 1 begins with a double slash (//) and is ignored by the translation system. Such lines are called comments and are meant for the reader of the program. They tell the user what the program is going to do. Comments begin with // and extend to the end of the line. Another way of entering comments into the program is to insert them between /* and */. Comments between /* and */ can extend across any number of lines.

Line 2 names the program or application class. Many systems require that the file name be the same as the class name with an extension attached. The class file in the disk with this manual all have the extension .java following the name of the class. Line 3 is the beginning brace that encloses the class.

Every Java application must have a method named main. Its heading must look exactly like line 4. Don't worry about what it means at the moment, just copy it exactly when you are writing your programs. Line 5 contains only one character: the left brace ({). This character begins a block that is the body of the function. The right brace (}) on line 25 is the closing brace of the block; it ends the body of the method. The body of the method contains the statements that are translated by the compiler and executed when the program is run.

Lines 6 through 11 instruct the compiler to assign the final identifier on the left of the equal sign a place in memory and to store the value on the right of the equal sign in that place. A final (or constant) declaration is made up of the reserved word final followed by a data type identifier or a class, in this case char or String. char says that the value to be stored in the constant is one alphanumeric character. String says that the value to be stored in the constant is a string of characters. The data type identifier or class name is followed by the name to be given to the constant. The constant name is followed by an equal sign and the value to be stored there. In line 6, a semicolon is stored in constant SEMI_COLON. In line 7, the string made up of the characters 'w', 'e', 'n', 't', and ' ' (blank) is stored in VERB1. Lines 8 through 11 define four more String constants. By convention, most Java programmers use all uppercase for constant identifiers.

Lines 12 through 15 contain the declarations of String variables. In line 12, firstLine is declared to be a String variable. The compiler assigns a memory location to firstLine. Nothing is stored in firstLine yet, but when values are stored there, they must be values of class String. In lines 13 through 15, String variables secondLine, thirdLine, and fourthLine are assigned memory locations.

Lines 16 through 19 are assignment statements. In an assignment statement, the expression on the right side of the equal sign is evaluated, and the result is stored in the variable whose identifier is on the left of the equal sign. In line 16, the expression is made up of a literal string constant, a named string constant, and another literal string constant. The operator that combines them is the *concatenation operator* (+). This binary operator takes two arguments. It appends the string on the right to the end of the string on the left. The result in line 16 is the string "The itsy bitsy spider went up the water spout". Lines 17 through 19 are evaluated the same way.

Lines 20 through 24 cause information to be written on the screen. Java provides System.out, an object that represents an output device, which is by default the screen. We can use the methods print and println to send messages to

System.out to print information on the screen. The information to be printed is enclosed in parentheses. The only difference between the two methods is that println prints an end-of-line before returning. Let's look at line 20 (repeated below) in detail.

```
20.     System.out.println(firstLine + SEMI_COLON);
```

Line 20 sends a message to object System.out, using the println method, which says to print the expression between the parentheses. To evaluate the expression, the first operand, firstLine, a String variable containing the string "The itsy bitsy spider went up the water spout", is concatenated with the constant semicolon character. The resulting string is written on the screen.

Line 21 prints the string "down came the rain and washed the spider out;" on the next line, because line 20 used method println rather than method print. Line 22 tells System.out to print the third line of the rhyme without the end-of-line symbol. Line 23 sends a message to print—print what? There is nothing between the parentheses. Line 23 uses method println, which always writes an end-of-line. Using println with nothing between the parentheses just writes the end-of-line symbol.

Line 24 sends a message to System.out to print the last line of the rhyme: "and the itsy bitsy spider went up the spout again." Note the syntax for these statements: the object, a dot, the method name, and a pair of parentheses. The values within the parentheses are called parameters.

We said that the executable part of the program is a method named main. Line 25 is the closing right brace that ends the body of method main and thus the executable part of the program. Line 26 is the closing right brace that ends the class that is the application. The output from this program is:

```
The itsy bitsy spider went up the water spout;
down came the rain and washed the spider out;
out came the sun and dried up all the rain;
and the itsy bitsy spider went up the spout again.
```

Data Type char

A data type is a set of values and a set of operations on these values. In the preceding program, we used the data type identifier char. Data type char describe one alphanumeric character: a letter, a digit, or a special symbol. Java uses the Unicode character set in which each char constant or variable takes up two bytes (16 bits) of storage. The Unicode character set can represent many more characters than we, in English, can ever use. Therefore we use a subset of Unicode that corresponds to the American Standard Code for Information Interchange (ASCII for short). To represent a literal character in a program, we enclose it in single quotes. The following are seven alphanumeric characters available in all character sets.

```
'A'   'a'   '0'   ' '   '*'   '$'   '9'
```

Although arithmetic operations are defined on alphanumeric characters in Java, such operations would not make any sense to us at this point. However, there is a collating sequence defined on each character set, so we can ask if one character comes before another character. We show how to do this in Laboratory 4.

In program `Rhyme`, we used a `char` constant (`SEMI_COLON`) and a `char` literal (a period).

Classes

In application `Rhyme`, we used five constants of class `String`, `VERB1`, `VERB2`, `VERB3`, `VERB4`, and `VERB5`. We also used four variables of class `String`, `firstLine`, `secondLine`, `thirdLine`, and `fourthLine`. Constants and variables of type `char` hold one alphanumeric character. If we want to store a sequence of characters, we declare a constant or variable to be of class `String`. We specify the characters in the string by putting them within double quotation marks. Notice that a `char` value is written within single quotation marks; a `String` value is within double quotation marks. Here are a few examples.

```
"blue sky"  "sun shine"  "I"  'I'
```

Note that `"I"` and `'I'` are different. The first is a `String` literal with one character; the second is a `char` literal.

Concatenation is an operation defined on variables, constants, or literals of class `String`. This binary operator (+ in Java) takes the string on the right of the operator and appends it to the string on the left of the operator. If one of the operands is not a string, it is automatically converted to a string before the concatenation takes place. The result of a concatenation operation is always a string.

In Java, an application is a class containing at least the method `main`. The statement

```
2. public class Rhyme
```

defines a class named `Rhyme`. Everything between Lines 3 and 27 is part of the class. Line 4 is the heading for method `main`, defined as part of the class. Every Java application is a class, but not all classes are applications. A class with the modifier `public` in front of it that contains a `public` method named `main` is an application. In the next few chapters, we introduce classes that are not applications.

Interactive Input

Interactive input occurs when a program outputs a direction to a user to input a data value. The program describes exactly how the data should be keyed in, waits for the user to input the data, and then reads in the data values. Let's examine this process in the context of the following interactive application. Again the lines are numbered in order to talk about them.

```
1. //*************************************************************
   // Application Holidays inputs the name of a holiday and a day
   // of the week and prints a message saying that the holiday is
   // on such and such a day this year.
   //*************************************************************
2. import java.io.*;                    //Package for stream readers
3. public class TestHoliday
4. {
5.    static class Holiday
6.    {
7.       String holiday;               // Name of a holiday
```

```
8.      String dayOfWeek;               // Day of the week

9.      public void getHoliday() throws IOException
10.     {
11.        BufferedReader inData;       //Input stream for strings
12.        inData =
              new BufferedReader(new InputStreamReader(System.in));
13.        System.out.println("Enter the name of a holiday: ");
14.        holiday = inData.readLine();
15.        System.out.println("Enter the day of the week on which "
              + holiday + " falls: ");
16.        dayOfWeek = inData.readLine();
17.     }

18.     public void printMessage()
19.     {
20.        System.out.println(holiday + " falls on " + dayOfWeek +
              " this year.");
21.     }
22.
23.  public static void main(String[] args) throws IOException
24.  {
25.     Holiday celebrate;
26.     celebrate = new Holiday();
27.     celebrate.getHoliday();
28.     celebrate.printMessage();
29.  }
30.}
```

As in the previous program, line 1 contains the comments describing what the application does. Line 2 imports the package containing the stream readers. import java.io.* means to import all of the classes and methods located in package java.io. System.out is imported automatically, but the stream readers must be explicitly imported.

Line 3 names the application class; line 4 is the opening bracket and line 30 is the closing bracket that enclose the body of class TestHoliday. Line 5 names an enclosed class Holiday, whose body is bracketed by lines 6 and 22. Notice that class Holiday is not marked public. There can only be one public class in any application.

Lines 7 and 8 each declare a variable of class String. Line 9 is the heading for a public method getHoliday. Because the method issues an input command, the expression throws IOException must be on the heading. Lines 10 and 17 enclose the body of this method. Line 11 declares an input stream of type BufferedReader, whose definition is found in the java.io.*. In order to get one of these stream readers, we must instantiate a BufferedReader object. Instantiate means to get an instance of a class, and we do so with the new operator. Let's look carefully at line 12, in which this instantiation occurs.

```
12.    inData = new BufferedReader(new InputStreamReader(System.in));
```

inData is the name of the stream reader from which we will read data. We get a stream reader by the phrase new BufferedReader(). BufferedReader is a constructor method as well as a class name, and it takes as a parameter an instance of class InputStreamReader. How do we get an instance? We use new. Thus new InputStreamReader(System.in)) creates an instance to be passed to the

BufferedReader constructor. What is System.in? System.in is a very primitive object defined in java.io.*. System.in is a predefined object of class InputStream; with it we can read data as a string of raw bytes. InputStreamReader converts the raw bytes to Unicode characters, and BufferedReader converts these characters to an object of class String.

A constructor is a special method with the same name as the class whose purpose is to be used with new to create an instance (object) of the class. Most classes must have constructors to instantiate instances of the class. Class String is an exception. As you can see in application Rhyme, we can store a literal string (one within double quotes) directly into a variable of class String. This is a short cut provided by the class because this class is used so frequently.

Line 13 issues a message to method println to write "Enter the name of a holiday: " on the screen. This statement is a prompt to the user to enter data. Line 14 reads in the string and stores it in holiday. readLine() is a method in class BufferedReader that reads in a string. inData is an instance of class BufferedReader, and the method readLine is applied to it by putting in the instance name, a dot, and the method name. readLine is a value returning instance method, meaning that it returns the string that is read, which is then stored in string variable holiday.

Line 15 prints another prompt, and Line 16 reads in the string that the user keys. Thus ends the processing of method getHoliday. Line 18 is the method heading for a method that writes a message on the screen. Lines 19 and 21 bracket the body of this method.

We said that every application must have a method named main whose heading is written in a certain way. Line 23 is the heading for the main method in this application. Notice that this method is not contained within class Holiday, but within class TestHoliday, the application class. Lines 24 and 29 bracket the body of main. Line 25 declares a variable of class Holiday, and line 26 instantiates the variable. Line 27 sends a message to method getHoliday to apply itself to variable celebrate. Line 28 sends a message to method printMessage to apply itself to variable celebrate. Here is a copy of the output from this application.

```
Enter the name of a holiday:
Thanksgiving
Enter the day of the week on which Thanksgiving falls:
Thursday
Thanksgiving falls on Thursday this year.
```

Operator Symbols

Here is a table of the Java operators defined in this chapter.

Operator	Meaning
+	Concatenation
=	Assignment; evaluate expression on right and store in the variable named on the left
. (dot)	Symbol used between an instance of a class and a class method; a message is sent to the method to apply itself to the class instance (object)
new	An operator that takes the class name (constructor) and returns an object of the class type

Words and Symbols with Special Meanings

Certain words have predefined meanings within the Java language; these are called *reserved words*. For example, the names of data types are reserved words. In program Rhyme, there are six reserved words: class, public, static, void, final, and char. char and class are the names of built-in data types; public and static are modifiers; void tells the compiler that a method does not return a value; and final directs the compiler to set up a constant. public allows others to access a class or method. In this case, it is the JVM that executes the program that must be able to access the class and method main. We cover modifier static when we need the construct later.

What about the other identifiers that are not ones we defined but are not reserved words? These are shown in the following table.

Identifier	Meaning
String	A class that is provided by the Java language that describes a sequence of characters
System.out	An object that Java provides that represents the screen
print()	A method that can be applied to object System.out; tells the object to write the expression that is in parentheses on the screen.
println()	Same as print() except it writes the end-of-line after writing the expression
java.io	A package containing classes relating to input and output
BufferedReader	A class in package java.io with methods to convert Unicode characters to a string
InputStreamReader	A class in package java.io with methods to convert raw bytes to Unicode characters
System.in	An object of StreamReader; returns a stream of raw bytes
readLine	A method that can be applied to an object of class BufferedReader; tells the object to input a line of text

Two slashes (//) signal that the characters from that point to the end of the line are comments and are to be ignored by the compiler. Characters written between /* and */ are also comments and are ignored by the compiler.

Semicolons terminate statements in the Java language. There are 19 semicolons in application Rhyme, so there are 19 statements in the program, all in the main method: 5 define String constants, 1 defines a char constant, four declare String variables, 4 are assignment operations, and 5 send messages to System.out to be printed.

Laboratory 2: Prelab Assignment

Name _____ Date _____

Section _____

Examine the following program and answer Exercises 1 through 5.

```java
// Program Lunch writes out the contents of a sandwich

public class Lunch
{
  public static void main(String[] args)
  {
    final String HAM = "ham";
    final String CHEESE = "cheese";
    final String LETTUCE = "lettuce";
    final String BREAD = "bread";

    String filling;
    String sandwich;

    filling = HAM + " and " + CHEESE + " with " + LETTUCE;
    sandwich = filling + " on white " + BREAD + '.';
    System.out.println("Filling : " + filling);
    System.out.println("Sandwich : " + sandwich);
  }
}
```

Exercise 1: What is written by program Lunch?

Exercise 2: List the identifiers that are defined in program Lunch.

Exercise 3: Which of these identifiers are named constants?

Exercise 4: List the literal constants.

Exercise 5: List the identifiers that are defined in sending a message to the screen and state their role in the process.

Exercise 6: How many objects (instances) are represented in this statement?

```
in = new BufferedReader(new InputStreamReader(System.in));
```

Exercise 7: Explain the meaning of the statement in the previous exercise.

Lesson 2-1: Check Prelab Exercises

Name _____ Date _____

Section _____

Exercise 1: Run program `Lunch` to check your answer to Prelab Exercise 1. Was your answer completely correct? If it was not, explain where you made your mistake.

Exercise 2: The identifiers are `HAM`, `CHEESE`, `LETTUCE`, `BREAD`, `filling`, `sandwich`, `main`, `Lunch`, and `args`.

Exercise 3: The named constants are `HAM`, `CHEESE`, `LETTUCE`, and `BREAD`.

Exercise 4: The literal string constants are `"` and `", "` with `", "` on white `", "Filling : "`, and `"Sandwich : "`. The literal character constant is `'.'`.

Exercise 5: `System.out` is the object representing the output device. `print` and `println` are methods that can be applied to the object; they send a message to the output object to print what is within the parentheses.

Exercise 6: There are three objects: `System.in`, an instance of class `InputStreamReader`, and an instance of class `BufferedReader`.

```
in = new BufferedReader (new InputStreamReader(System.in));
```

Exercise 7: This statement instantiates an object of class `BufferedReader`. In order to do this, a class of `InputStreamReader` must be instantiated and passed as a parameter to the `BufferedReader` constructor. Object `System.in` (a parameter to the `InputStreamReader` constructor) inputs raw bytes. `InputStreamReader` converts these bytes to Unicode characters. `BufferedReader` converts the Unicode characters to an object of class `String`.

Lesson 2-2: Components of a Program

Name _____ Date _____

Section _____

This lesson uses program `Greet`. Compile and rerun the program after each modification.

```
// Program Greet prints a greeting on the screen

_____ class Greet
{
  public _____  _____ main(String[] args)
    ____
      _____String FIRST_NAME __ "Sarah ";
      final _____ LAST_NAME = "Sunshine";
      String message;
      _____ name;

      name __ FIRST_NAME __ LAST_NAME;
      message = "Good morning" __ ' ' + name + '.';
      System.out._____(message);
    ____
}
```

Exercise 1: Program `Greet` prints a greeting on the screen. However, it is missing certain identifiers, reserved words, and operators that are necessary for it to compile. Replace each blank with the appropriate identifier, reserved word, or operator and run the program. Record the output below.

Exercise 2: Replace the named constants with your first and last names and rerun the program.

Exercise 3: Make the greeting a named constant rather than a literal constant and rerun the program.

Exercise 4: Change the action part of the program so that the greeting is written on one line and your name is on the next line.

Lesson 2–3: Sending Information to the Output Stream

Name _____ Date _____

Section _____

Lesson 2-3 focuses on constructing output statements. Program `Shell` is the outline of a program. Use this shell for Exercises 1 through 3.

```
// Program Shell

public class Shell
{
  public static void main(String[] args)
  {

  }
}
```

Exercise 1: Write a program to print the following information single spaced on the screen. Use literal constants in the output statements themselves for each of the data items to be written on the screen. Run your program to verify that the output is as specified.

a. Your name (last name, comma, blank, first name)
b. Today's date (month:day:year)

Exercise 2: Change your program so that there is a space between the two lines of output. Compile and run your program.

Exercise 3: Change your program so that your first name is printed, followed by your last name with a blank in between. Compile and run your program.

Lesson 2-4: Reading Data Interactively

Name _____   Date _____

Section _____

Lesson 2-4 focuses on constructing an interactive dialog with a user. Each exercise asks you to fill in parts of a class or method. The last exercise asks you to put all the parts together into an application.

Exercise 1: Fill in the blanks in the following method (in file `getName`).

```
public void getName() _____
{
  in = new BufferedReader(_____);
  System.out.println("Enter name:");
  name = _____;__
}
```

Exercise 2: Fill in the blanks in the following method (in file `getMessage`).

```
public void getMessage() throws IOException
{
  System.out.println("Enter message:");
  message = _____;
}
```

Exercise 3: Fill in the blanks in the following method `printMessage` (in file `printMessage`).

```
public void printMessage()
{
  System.out.print("Hello " + _____);
  System.out.println(message);
}
```

Exercise 4: Fill in the blanks in the following method `main` (in file `main`).

```
public static void main(_____)throwsIOException

{
  Message text;
  text = new _____;
  text._____();
  text.getMessage___;
  _____.printMessage();
}
```

Exercise 5: Fill in the blanks in class Message (in file `Message`).

```
static class Message
{
   String _____;
   String _____;
   BufferedReader in;
   // Class methods follow.
}
```

Exercise 6: Fill in the pieces from exercises 1-5 into `TestMessage`. Compile and run application TestMessage.

```
import java.io.*;
public class TestMessage
{
   // Fill in the body using results of exercises 1-5
}
```

Lesson 2-5: Debugging

Exercise 1: Program `Dinner` (on file `Dinner.java`) writes a dinner menu. Compile and run this program. Be forewarned: Bugs are lurking in the code. The lines of the program are numbered on the right in comments. Fill in the following chart, showing the errors and what you did to correct them. (This time you do not get a printed copy; you must use the file only.) If the errors are caused by missing code, explain in the Corrections column.

#	OK	Error	Corrections (if error)
1			
2			
3			
4			
5			
6			
7			
8			
9			
10			
11			
12			
13			
14			
15			
16			
17			

Exercise 2: Program `Dinner2` contains a syntactically correct version of program `Dinner`, but the output is not correct. What must you do to correct this problem?

Postlab Activities

Exercise 1: Write a program to print out the following lines from Dr. Seuss's *Horton Hatches the Egg*.[1]

I meant what I said
and I said what I meant
An elephant's faithful
one hundred percent

Put a border of asterisks around the entire quotation (all four sides). Each line of the quotation should be sent to the output stream in the same statement.

Exercise 2: Write a program that produces a cover sheet for your laboratory assignments. It should have the chapter number, the lessons that have been assigned, your instructor's name, your name, the date, and any other information that your instructor has requested.

Exercise 3: Write a program that writes a birthday message to your mother. Surround the message with asterisks.

Exercise 4: Write a program that reads in a name and writes a birthday message.

---

[1] Dr. Seuss, *Horton Hatches the Egg* (New York: Random House, 1940).

Arithmetic Expressions

- To be able to write simple arithmetic expressions to accomplish a specified task.

- To be able to convert a value from one numeric type to another numeric type.

- To be able to write output statements that format data in specified ways.

- To be able to use value-returning library methods.

- To be able to use string methods to manipulate string data.

- To be able to convert a string to a numeric type.

- To be able to declare a class with methods.

- To be able to debug a program with syntax errors.

- To be able to debug a program with logic errors.

Laboratory 3: Assignment Cover Sheet

Name _____ Date _____

Section _____

Fill in the following table showing which exercises have been assigned for each lesson and check what you are to submit: (1) lab sheets, (2) listings of output files, and/or (3) listings of code. Your instructor or teaching assistant (TA) can use the Completed column for grading purposes.

Activities	Assigned: Check or list exercise numbers	Submit (1) (2) (3)			Completed
Prelab					
Review					
Prelab Assignment					
Inlab					
Lesson 3-1: Check Prelab Exercises					
Lesson 3-2: Arithmetic Operations					
Lesson 3-3: Formatting Output					
Lesson 3-4: Value-returning Mathematical Methods					
Lesson 3-5: String Methods					
Lesson 3-6: Classes and Methods					
Lesson 3-7: Debugging					
Postlab					

Prelab Activities

Review

Java's data types are divided into two main categories: primitive types and reference types. The variables in these two categories differ in how they are stored in memory. `char` variables and variables of the numeric types we discuss in this chapter are primitive types and are stored in the location assigned to the variable. Variables of class `String` and other classes are reference types; the values of reference types are stored in another place in memory with a pointer to their location stored in the variable name. In this chapter, we examine the rest of the primitive types with the exception of type `boolean`, which we cover in Laboratory 4.

Numeric Types

In Java, there are four integral types that can be used to refer to an integer value: `byte`, `short`, `int`, and `long`. These types represent integers of different sizes, ranging from 8 bits to 64 bits. `int` is the most common data type used for integer values. A variable of type `int` can hold a value in the range -2147483648 through $+2147483647$. `float` and `double` are data type identifiers that refer to floating-point numbers; that is, numbers with a whole and a fractional part. Integer literals are assumed to be of type `int`; floating-point literals are assumed to be of type `double`.

Variables and constants of integral and floating-point types can be combined into expressions using arithmetic operators. The operations between constants or variables of these types are addition (+), subtraction (-), multiplication (*), and division (/). If the operands of the division operation are integral, the result is the integral quotient. If the operands are floating-point types, the result is a floating-point type with the division carried out to as many decimal places as the type allows. There is an additional operator, the modulus operator (%), that returns the remainder from division. If the arguments to the modulus operator are integral, the result is integral.

In addition to the standard arithmetic operators, Java provides an *increment* operator and a *decrement* operator. The increment operator ++ adds one to its operand; the decrement operator -- subtracts one from its operand. The increment and decrement operators can be either postfix operators or prefix operators. We only use them as postfix operators in this text.

Precedence Rules

The precedence rules of arithmetic apply to arithmetic expressions in a program. That is, the order of execution of an expression that contains more than one operation is determined by the precedence rules of arithmetic. These rules state that parentheses have the highest precedence; multiplication, division, and modulus have the next highest precedence; and addition and subtraction have the lowest precedence. Because parentheses have the highest precedence, they can be used to change the order in which operations are executed. The Java postfix increment and decrement operators have the highest precedence of any of the arithmetic operators.

When operators of the same precedence are combined, they are usually evaluated from left to right. See appendix B for more information.

Converting Numeric Types

If an integral and a floating-point variable or constant are mixed in an operation, the integral value is changed temporarily to its equivalent floating-point representation before the operation is executed. This automatic conversion of an integral value to a floating-point value is called *type coercion*. Type coercion also occurs when a floating-point value is assigned to an integral variable. Coercion from an integer to a floating point is exact. Although the two values are represented differently in memory, both representations are exact. However, when a floating-point value is coerced into an integral value, loss of information occurs unless the floating-point value is a whole number. That is, 1.0 can be coerced into 1, but what about 1.5? Is it coerced into 1 or 2? In Java when a floating-point value is coerced into an integral value, the floating-point value is truncated. Thus, the floating-point value 1.5 is coerced into 1.

Type changes can be made explicit by placing the name of the new type in parentheses before the value to be changed. That is,

```
intValue = 10.66;
```

and

```
intValue = (int)10.66;
```

produce the same results. The first is implicit; the second is explicit. Explicit type changing is called *type casting* or *type conversion*, as opposed to implicit type changing, which is called *type coercion*. Explicit type conversion is more self-documenting and is therefore better style.[1]

Value-Returning Mathematical Methods

Java provides a collection of preprogrammed mathematical methods in class `Math`. The class includes such useful methods as `Math.cos` and `Math.sin`, which calculate the cosine and sine of a variable in radians, `Math.pow`, which raises a value to a power, and `Math.sqrt`, which takes the square root of a floating-point value. These methods are all *value-returning* methods and are executed by using their names in an expression. The value that is returned replaces the method name in the expression. Here is an example.

```
System.out.println("" + Math.pow(3.0, 4.0) + Math.sqrt(81.0));
```

`Math.pow(3.0, 4.0)` returns the value `81.0`; this value is written on the screen. `Math.sqrt(81.0)` returns the value `9.0`, which is written on the screen. The values in the parentheses to the right of the method names are called *parameters* to the

---

[1] Although this terminology is standard, Java uses type conversion for both implicit and explicit conversions.

method. Parameters are the values that the methods use as input. In the case of `Math.pow`, the first value is the one to be taken to a power and the second is the power. The parameter to `Math.sqrt` is the value for which the square root is calculated. Note that we begin the output expression with the empty string (" ") in order to concatenate it with the floating-point value returned from `Math.pow`. The result is a string, which is then concatenated with the floating-point value from `Math.sqrt`.

You can write your own value-returning methods as well. Look at the following program.

```
// Program Miles prints miles in kilometers
public class Miles
{
  // Value-returning method
  public static double kilometers(int miles)
  {
    final double KILOMETERS_PER_MILE = 1.609;
    return KILOMETERS_PER_MILE * (double)miles;
  }

  public static void main(String[] args)
  {
    System.out.println("One mile is " + kilometers(1)
        + " kilometers.");
    System.out.println("Ten miles is " + kilometers(10)
        + " kilometers.");
    System.out.println("One hundred miles is "
        + kilometers(100) + " kilometers.");
  }
}
```

Method `kilometers` is a user-defined value-returning method. It takes one `int` parameter that represents miles and returns that value expressed in kilometers. Method `kilometers` is invoked by using its name in an output statement. That is, the value returned from the method is sent to the output stream.

Void Methods

Java provides another type of method called a *void method*. A void method is the name of an action that does not return a single value. Value-returning methods have the data type of the value being returned before the name of the method. Void methods have the word `void` before the name of the method to indicate that they are not returning a single value. Rather than being used in an expression, void methods are used as statements in the body of other methods.

More about Strings

In Laboratory 2, we introduced the binary operation concatenation, which we used to combine strings and characters. Class `String` provides three additional operations that are very useful when working with character data. They are `length`, `indexOf`, and `substring`. Let's examine their syntax and semantics in the context of the following application.

```
// Program StrDemo demonstrates string methods.
import java.io.*;
public class StrDemo
{
  public static void main(String[] args) throws IOException
  {
    BufferedReader inData;     //Input stream for strings
    inData = new BufferedReader(new InputStreamReader(System.in));
    int dollars;
    String inLine;
    String dollarsInString;
    final String CAT = "cat";

    System.out.println("Enter a string.");
    inLine = inData.readLine();
    // Examples of various string operations

    System.out.println(inLine.length());
    System.out.println(inLine.indexOf("the"));
    System.out.println(inLine.indexOf(CAT));
    System.out.println(inLine.substring(17, 23));
    System.out.println(inLine.substring(17, 17));
    System.out.println(inLine.substring(17, 23).length());
    System.out.println("" + inLine.charAt(0) + inLine.charAt(1));
    System.out.println("How much would you would pay " +
      "for the doggie?");
    dollarsInString = inData.readLine();
    dollars = Integer.parseInt(dollarsInString);
    System.out.println("Would you really pay $" + dollars + "?");
    inData.close();
  }
}
```

Output:

Line	Appears in window
1.	Enter a string.
2.	How much is that doggie in the window?
3.	38
4.	27
5.	-1
6.	doggie
7.	
8.	6
9.	Ho
10.	How much would you would pay for the doggie?
11.	443
12.	Would you really pay $443?

The lines of output are numbered so that we can talk about them. The first line of output is the prompt for the user to enter a string. The second is the line keyed by the user. The third line of output is 38, the number of characters in the string entered by the user. length is a method that is applied to an object of type String using *dot notation*: the name of the String object, followed by a dot (period), followed by the name of the method. length is a value-returning method, so it is used in an expression. Although it does not have any parameters, it still must have parentheses to the right of the name.

Method indexOf looks for its argument in the string to which it is applied. The fourth line of output is 13. "the" is found in inLine beginning at the 13th position. How can that be? The "t" in "the" is the 14th character. Yes, well most humans start counting with one, but Java begins counting with zero. "H" is in the zeroth position, making "the" start in the 13th position. The fifth line of output shows what happens when the string (or character) being searched for does not occur in the string object: A –1 is returned.

The next four lines demonstrate what the substring method does. It returns a substring of the object to which it is applied, beginning at the position specified by the first parameter. The ending position plus one of the substrings is specified in the second parameter. Therefore, if we subtract the first parameter from the second parameter, we get the length of the substring, which is demonstrated in the sixth line. The seventh line shows what happens if the two parameters are the same: The empty string is returned. If either parameter is beyond the end of the string or the second parameter is smaller than the first, an error results. One way to avoid such an error is to use the minimum method in class Math. If you want the substring beginning at start and ending at end - 1, use the following expression to avoid an error.

```
inLine.substring(start, Math.min(end, inLine.length());
```

The eighth line demonstrates that a method can be applied to the result of another method. The ninth line demonstrates the charAt method, which returns the character at the position specified in the parameter.

In Laboratory 2, we introduced interactive input, saying that method readLine inputs a line of text and returns it as a string. What if we want to input a numeric value rather than a string? Each of the numeric types has a special method that takes a string and converts it to a value of the numeric type. Let's look carefully at the last few lines in this application.

```
System.out.println("How much would you would pay " +
  "for the doggie?");
dollarsInString = inData.readLine();
dollars = Integer.parseInt(dollarsInString);
System.out.println("Would you really pay $" +
  dollars + "?");
```

The first line prints a prompt to the screen asking how much would the user pay for the doggie. The next line reads in a string. The third line converts the string to an integer value. parseInt is a class method of class Integer that converts the string parameter into a value of type int.

Each built-in numeric type has a class associated with it that contains methods and constants that can be used when working with the type. The class associated with type int is Integer. The class for each of the other types is the same as the type name, but beginning with an uppercase letter. If you were to enter a real value instead of an integer value, an IOException would occur.

Output Formatting

We can control the vertical spacing of lines on the screen (or page) by using `println`. For example, the first of the following statements creates three blank lines and writes the message "Happy New Year" on the fourth line.

```
System.out.println();
System.out.println();
System.out.println();
System.out.print("Happy New Year");
System.out.println("!");
```

Where does the exclamation point go? Immediately following the *r* in *Year*. Characters are streamed to `System.out` without line breaks unless an end-of-line is inserted into the stream by using `println`.

We can put blanks in a line by including them within the strings that we are writing. For example, we can put extra blanks before and after the message as follows:

```
System.out.print(  "  Happy New Year  ");
```

Note that we also added extra blanks before the first double quote. These extra blanks have no effect on the output whatsoever. Only blanks within the strings are sent to `System.out`.

Operator Symbols

Here is a table showing the Java equivalent of the standard arithmetic operators and the other operations defined in this laboratory.

Operator	Meaning
+	Unary plus
-	Unary minus
+	Addition
-	Subtraction
*	Multiplication
/	Floating-point operands: floating-point result
	Integer operands: quotient
	Mixed operands: floating-point result
%	Modulus (remainder from division)
++	Increment by one; can be prefix or postfix; as postfix, has highest precedence.

Operator	Meaning
--	Decrement by one; can be prefix or postfix; as postfix, has highest precedence.
length	A method that returns the length of the object to which it is applied.
indexOf	A method that searches the string object to which it is applied looking for a character or string specified in its parameter; returns the beginning position if a match is found and –1 otherwise.
substring	A method that returns a substring of the object to which it is applied beginning at the position specified in the first parameter and continuing until the character in the position before the second parameter has been added to the substring. If either parameter specifies a position outside the string or if the second parameter is smaller than the first, an error occurs.
parseInt	A class method of class Integer that takes a string parameter and returns it as the corresponding int value.
parseDouble	A class method of class Double that takes a string parameter and returns it as the corresponding double value.

Laboratory 3: Prelab Assignment

Name _____ Date _____

Section _____

Exercise 1: Show what is written by each of the output statements in the following program.

```java
// Program Pres demonstrates the precedence of operators

public class Pres
{
  public static void main(String[] args)
  {
    System.out.println(4 + 3 * 5);
    System.out.println((4 + 3) * 5);
    System.out.println(4 * 5 % 3 + 2));
    System.out.println(4 * (5 / 3) + 2);
  }
}
```

Examine the following program carefully and then answer the questions in Exercises 2, 3, and 4.

```java
// Program Mixed demonstrates more on precedence of operators
//   and what happens in mixed-mode  arithmetic
public class Mixed
{ public static void main(String[] args)
  {
    float  fltValue;
    fltValue = (float)3.14159;

    int intValue;
    intValue = 5;

    System.out.println("" + intValue / intValue);
    System.out.println("" + (float) intValue / intValue);
```

```
      intValue++;
    System.out.println("" + intValue % 4);
    System.out.println("" + intValue);
    System.out.println("" + 2066 % 1066);
    System.out.println("" + 2066.0 % 1066.0);
    System.out.println("" + 2066 / intValue);

    System.out.println("" + fltValue / intValue);
    intValue = (int)(fltValue + intValue);
    System.out.println("" + intValue);
    fltValue = (float) intValue;
    System.out.println("" + fltValue / intValue);
    System.out.println("" + fltValue/ (float)intValue );
  }
}
```

Class Pres does not explicitly convert the results to strings by concatenating them with an empty string before printing them. Class Mixed does the explicit conversion. With System.out.println, either is correct.

Exercise 2: Show what is written by each of the output statements.

Exercise 3: What statement contains a type coercion?

Exercise 4: What statement contains a type conversion?

Lesson 3-1: Check Prelab Exercises

Name _____ Date _____

Section _____

Exercise 1: Run program `Pres` to check your answers. Were your answers completely correct? If they were not, explain what was wrong.

Exercise 2: Run program `Mixed` to check your answers. Were your answers completely correct? If they were not, explain what was wrong.

Exercise 3: Implicit conversion.
```
System.out.println("" + fltValue / intValue);
```

Exercise 4: Explicit conversion.
```
System.out.println("" + fltValue/ (float)intValue);
```

Lesson 3-2: Arithmetic Operations

Name _____ Date _____

Section _____

Use program Convert for Exercises 1 through 6. Study this program carefully. It converts a temperature from Fahrenheit to Celsius and a temperature from Celsius to Fahrenheit.

```java
// Application Convert converts a temperature in Fahrenheit to
//  Celsius and a temperature in Celsius to Fahrenheit
import java.io.*;
public class Convert
{
  public static void main(String[] args) throws IOException
  {
    BufferedReader inData =
      new BufferedReader(new InputStreamReader(System.in));

    int fToC; // Place to store Celsius answer
    int cToF; // Place to store the Fahrenheit answer

    System.out.println("Enter a value to be converted "
      + " from Fahrenheit to Celsius.");
    fToC = Integer.parseInt(inData.readLine());

    System.out.println(fToC + " in Fahrenheit is "
      + (5 * (fToC - 32)/9) + " in Celsius. ");
  }
}
```

Exercise 1: Compile and run program Convert. What value did you input and what is written out for fToC?

Exercise 2: Notice that the application declares two values (cToF and fToC) but only inputs, calculates, and prints one value fToC. Add the statements to calculate and print cToF. The formula is 9 times the temperature in Celsius divided by 5 plus 32. Compile and run the application.

What values did you input and what values were written?

Exercise 3: Run your program four times using the following input values. Record the values for fToC and cToF for each set of values.

Fahrenheit	Celsius	fToC	cToF	
a. 212	100	_____	_____	
b. 100	50	_____	_____	
c. 122	37	_____	_____	
d. _____	_____	_____	_____	(You choose.)

Exercise 4: Examine the output from b and c. The results seem to be inconsistent. Describe the inconsistency and make a hypothesis to explain it.

Exercise 5: Change the integer variables to type double and rerun the application with the same data you used in parts b and c in Exercise 3. Do the results confirm your hypothesis? Explain.

Exercise 6: Remove the parentheses from both assignment statements and rerun the application using the values that you used in part c in Exercise 3.

What values are printed?   fToC _____ cToF _____

These values are not the same ones that were printed in Exercise 5. Why?

Lesson 3-3: Formatting Output

Name _____ Date _____

Section _____

Use the following program `Shell` for Exercises 1 and 2.

```
// Program Shell
public class Shell
{
  public static void main(String[] args)
  {

  }
}
```

Exercise 1: Add the statements necessary to print the following strings centered in fields of 20 characters all on one line: "Good Morning", "Monika", and "Moonlight!" Compile and run your program; show your output.

Good morning
Monika
Moonlight

Exercise 2: Change the program in Exercise 1 so that the three strings print on three separate lines with a blank line in between each string.

Lesson 3-4: Value-Returning Mathematical Methods

Name _____   Date _____

Section _____

Use the following shell for Exercises 1 and 2.

```
// Program Method demonstrates the use of library and
//  user-defined methods

public class Method
{
  static double answer(double one, double two, double three)
  {
    // Do you recognize this formula?
    return ((- two + Math.sqrt(Math.pow(two,_____)
        - (4.0 * one * three))) / (2.0 * one));
  }

  public static void main(String[] args)
  {
    System.out.println("" + answer(_____,_____,_____));
  }
}
```

Exercise 1: Fill in the blanks in method `answer` such that the value stored in parameter `two` is taken to the second power. Fill in the blanks in method `main` so that method `answer` is invoked with `10.0` as the first parameter, `20.0` as the second parameter, and `5.0` as the third parameter. What is printed?

Exercise 2: Change the program in Exercise 1 so that method `answer` is invoked with `5.0` as the first parameter, `20.0` as the second parameter, and `10.0` as the third parameter. What is printed?

Exercise 3: Change the program in Exercise 1 so that method `answer` is invoked with `5.0` as the first parameter, `10.0` as the second parameter, and `20.0` as the third parameter. What happens? Explain why.

Lesson 3-5: String Methods

Name _____ Date _____

Section _____

Use the following program Shell for Exercises 1 through 3.

```
// Program ShellStr
import java.io.*;
public class ShellStr
{ public static void main(String[] args)
   {

   }
}
```

Exercise 1: Prompt for and read a string made up of your first and last name with a blank in between. Write out your string followed by a statement saying how many characters were in the string. Label your output appropriately. Compile and run your program. What was printed?

Exercise 2: Add the statements to the program in Exercise 1 to print your name, last name first, followed by a comma and your first name. Use methods indexOf and substring to accomplish this task. Compile and run your program. What is printed?

Exercise 3: Add the statements to the previous program to print your last name, followed by a comma and your first initial. Use methods indexOf and substring to accomplish this task. Compile and run your program. What is printed?

Lesson 3-6: Classes and Methods

Name _____ Date _____

Section _____

Use the following application `Shell` for Exercises 1 through 4.

```
// Application CarDr test a class that represents a car.
import java.io.*;
public class CarDr
{
  static class Car
  {
    // Car class variables go here
    // Car class methods go here
  }
  public static void main(String[] args)
  {
    // Statements that manipulate Car class go here
  }
}
```

Exercise 1: Add statements to this shell that declare three variables: `make`, `cost`, and `numDoors`.

Exercise 2: Add a method to class `Car` to prompt for and read values into the variables.

Exercise 3: Add a method that prints out the values of the variables, properly labeled.

Exercise 4: Add a method `main` to class `CarDr` that declares and instantiates a `Car` object, calls the method from Exercise 2 to read in the values, and calls the method from Exercise 3 to write out the values. Compile and run your program. What were your input values? What was the output?

Lesson 3–7: Debugging

Name _____ Date _____

Section _____

Exercise 1: Program Typos contains syntax errors. Correct the program, describe the errors, and show what is printed.

List the syntax errors.

Show what is printed.

Exercise 2: The output from program Typos looks strange! Clearly, there are logic bugs lurking in the code. Find and correct these errors.

List the logic errors.

Show what is printed.

Exercise 3: Program `Ounces` converts a value in ounces to cups, quarts, and gallons. Compile and run this program. Be forewarned: A few bugs are lurking in the code. The elements (definitions, statements, and symbols) of the program are numbered on the left in comments. Fill in the following chart, listing the syntax errors and showing what you did to correct them.

#	OK	Error	Corrections (if error)
1			
2			
3			
4			
5			
6			
7			
8			
9			
10			
11			
12			
13			
14			
15			
16			

Exercise 4: Now that program `Ounces` compiles and runs, you must check the output for logic errors. List the logic errors that you find and indicate what you did to correct them. Run your corrected program.

Exercise 5: Did you double-check the answers to be sure they were reasonable? Compare your solution to program `Ounces2`. Did you find all the logic errors?

Postlab Activities

Exercise 1: Write a program that prints the hundreds digit in a series of integer constants. For example, if constants ONE and TWO are 1456 and 254, respectively, your program should print 4 and 2. You may choose the integers yourself. Your output should include the original number followed by the digit in the hundreds position. Label your output appropriately.

Exercise 2: Write a program that prints the number 1349.9431 with three decimal places, with two decimal places, and with one decimal place. (*Hint*: Use / and %.)

Exercise 3: Write a program that prints each of the following values in two columns: 1234, 45, 7, 87, 99999. The first column is left-justified and the second column is right-justified.

Exercise 4: Write a program that takes a string of thirty hash marks (#) and prints six hash marks on five lines with a blank line in between. The variable that originally contains the thirty hash marks should contain the empty string at the end of your program.

Exercise 5: Much has been said about how overweight much of the American population is today. Write a design and a program that prompts the user to enter his or her weight in pounds and his or her height in inches. The program calculates the body mass index (BMI) and writes it on System.out. The formula is

$$BMI = weight * 703 / (height*height)$$

Conditions, Logical Expressions, and Selection Control Structures

■ To be able to construct Boolean expressions to evaluate a given condition.

■ To be able to construct *if* statements to perform a specified task.

■ To be able to construct *if-else* statements to perform a specified task.

■ To be able to construct nested *if* statements to perform a specified task.

■ To be able to design and implement a test plan.

■ To be able to debug a program with a selection control structure.

Laboratory 4: Assignment Cover Sheet

Name _____   Date _____

Section _____

Fill in the following table showing which exercises have been assigned for each lesson and check what you are to submit: (1) lab sheets, (2) listings of output files, and/or (3) listings of code. Your instructor or teaching assistant (TA) can use the Completed column for grading purposes.

Activities	Assigned: Check or list exercise numbers	Submit (1) (2) (3)			Completed
Prelab					
Review					
Prelab Assignment					
Inlab					
Lesson 4-1: Check Prelab Exercises					
Lesson 4-2: Boolean Expressions					
Lesson 4-3: *if* Statements					
Lesson 4-4: *if-else* Statements					
Lesson 4-5: Nested Logic					
Lesson 4-6: Test Plan					
Postlab					

Prelab Activities

Review

The physical order of a program is the order in which the statements are *listed*. The logical order of a program is the order in which the statements are *executed*. In this chapter, you learn to ask questions in your program and change the order in which the statements are executed depending on the answers to your questions.

Boolean Data Type

To ask a question in a program, you make a statement. If your statement is true, the answer to the question is yes. If your statement is not true, the answer to the question is no. You make these statements in the form of *Boolean expressions*. A Boolean expression asserts (states) that something is true. The assertion is evaluated and if it is true, the Boolean expression is true. If the assertion is not true, the Boolean expression is false.

In Java, data type `boolean` is used to represent Boolean data. Each `boolean` constant or variable can contain one of two values: `true` or `false`.

Boolean Expressions

A Boolean expression can be a simple Boolean variable or constant or a more complex expression involving one or more of the relational operators. Relational operators take two operands and test for a relationship between them. The following table shows the relational operators and the Java symbols that stand for them.

Java Symbol	Relationship
==	Equal to
!=	Not equal to
>	Greater than
<	Less than
>=	Greater than or equal to
<=	Less than or equal to

For example, the Boolean expression

```
number1 < number2
```

is evaluated to `true` if the value stored in `number1` is less than the value stored in `number2`, and evaluated to `false` otherwise.

When a relational operator is applied between variables of type `char`, the assertion is in terms of where the two operands fall in the collating sequence of a particular character set. Java uses the Unicode character set, of which ASCII is a subset. The ASCII character set is in the Appendix. For example,

```
character1 < character2
```

is evaluated to `true` if the character stored in `character1` comes before the character stored in `character2` in the collating sequence.

Although we can apply the relational operators equal and not equal to values of class `String`, we don't get the answer we expect. Recall that a reference variable does not actually contain an object of the class, but the *address* of an object. We have not used the `new` operator with `Strings` because we have stored literal strings and the system takes care of instantiating the string for us. As a consequence of the way strings are stored, if we use the relational operators, we are asking if the two variables contain pointers to the same string. If we want to find out if two strings contain the same values, we must use methods defined in the `String` class. Four useful ones are shown below.

String class

Method	Parameter	Returns	Function
equals	String	boolean	Returns `true` if the `String` instance to which the method is applied is equal to the `String` parameter.
compareTo	String	int	Returns a negative integer if the `String` instance comes before the parameter (alphabetically); 0 if the strings are identical; and a positive integer if the `String` instance comes after the `String` parameter.
toLowerCase		String	Returns an identical string with all the uppercase letters converted to lowercase.
toUpperCase		String	Returns an identical string with all the lowercase letters converted to uppercase.

It is useful to convert strings to all uppercase or to all lowercase before comparing them.

We must be careful when applying the relational operators to floating-point operands, particularly equal (`==`) and not equal (`!=`). Integer values can be represented exactly; floating-point values with fractional parts often are not exact in the low-order decimal places. Therefore, you should compare floating-point values for near equality.

A simple Boolean expression is either a Boolean variable or constant or an expression involving the relational operators that evaluates to either true or false. These simple Boolean expressions can be combined using the logical operations defined on Boolean values. There are three Boolean operators: AND, OR, and NOT. Here is a table showing the meaning of these operators and the symbols that are used to represent them in Java.

Java Symbol	*Meaning*
&&	AND is a binary Boolean operator. If both operands are true, the result is true. Otherwise, the result is false.
||	OR is a binary Boolean operator. If at least one of the operands is true, the result is true. Otherwise, if both are false, the result is false.
!	NOT is a unary Boolean operator. NOT changes the value of its operand: If the operand is true, the result is false; if the operand is false, the result is true.

If relational operators and Boolean operators are combined in the same expression in Java, the Boolean operator NOT (!) has the highest precedence, the relational operators have next higher precedence, and the Boolean operators AND (&&) and OR (\|\|) come last (in that order). Expressions in parentheses are always evaluated first.

For example, given the following expression (`stop` is a `boolean` variable)

```
!stop || ((count <= 10) && (sum >= limit))
```

`!stop` is evaluated first, the expressions involving the relational operators are evaluated next, the `&&` is applied, and finally the `||` is applied. Java uses *short-circuit evaluation*. The evaluation is done in left-to-right order and halts as soon as the result is known. For example, in the above expression, if `!stop` is true the evaluation stops because the left operand to the OR operation (`||` operator) is true. There is no reason to evaluate the rest of the expression: true OR anything is true. If `!stop` is false, then the right side must be evaluated, beginning with `(count <= 10)`.

The following table summarizes the precedence of all the Java operators we have seen so far.

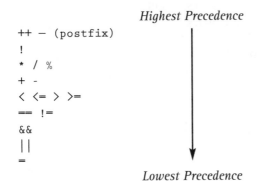

Highest Precedence

```
++ - (postfix)
!
* / %
+ -
< <= > >=
== !=
&&
||
=
```

Lowest Precedence

if and if-else Statements

The *if* statement allows the programmer to change the logical order of a program; that is, make the order in which the statements are executed differ from the order in which they are listed in the program.

The *if* statement uses a Boolean expression to determine whether to execute a statement or to skip it.

```
if (number < 0)
  number = 0;
sum = sum + number;
```

The expression (number < 0) is evaluated. If the result is true, the statement number = 0 is executed. If the result is false, the statement is skipped. In either case, the next statement to be executed is sum = sum + number. The statement that is either executed or skipped may be a *block*. A block is a group of statements in the action part of the program enclosed in braces.

The *if-else* statement uses a Boolean expression to determine which of two statements to execute.

```
System.out.print("Today is a ");
if (temperature <= 32)
  System.out.print("cold ");
else
  System.out.print("nice ");
System.out.println("day.");
```

The characters "Today is a " are sent to System.out. The expression (temperature <= 32) is evaluated. If the result is true, the characters "cold " are sent to System.out. If the result is false, the characters "nice " are sent to System.out. In either case, the next statement to be executed sends the characters "day." to System.out. Either of the statements may be a block (compound statement) as shown in the following example.

```
if (temperature <= 32)
{
  System.out.println("Today is a cold day.");
  System.out.println("Sitting by the fire is appropriate.");
}
else
{
    System.out.println("Today is a nice day.");
    System.out.println("How about taking a walk?");
}
```

There is a point of Java syntax that you should note: There is never a semicolon after the right brace of a block (compound statement).

Nested Logic

An *if* statement uses a Boolean expression to determine whether to execute a statement or skip it. An *if-else* statement uses a Boolean expression to determine which of two statements to execute. The statements to be executed or skipped can be simple statements or blocks (compound statements). There is no constraint on what the statements can be. This means that the statement to be skipped in an *if* statement can be another *if* statement. In the *if-else* statement, either or both of the choices can be another *if* statement. An *if* statement within another *if* statement is called a *nested if* statement.

The following is an example of a nested *if* statement.

```
System.out.print("Today is a ");
if (temperature <= 32)
   System.out.print("cold ");
else if (temperature <= 85)
   System.out.print("nice ");
else
   System.out.print("hot ");
System.out.println("day.");
```

in between

Notice that the nested *if* statement does not have to ask if the temperature is greater than 32 because we do not execute the `else` branch of the first *if* statement if the temperature is less than or equal to 32.

In nested *if* statements, there may be confusion as to which `if` an `else` belongs. In the absence of braces, the compiler pairs an `else` with the most recent `if` that doesn't have an `else`. You can override this pairing by enclosing the preceding `if` in braces to make the clause of the outer *if* statement complete.

Test Plans

How do you test a specific program to determine its correctness? You design and implement a *test plan*. A test plan for a program is a document that specifies the test cases that should be run, the reason for each test case, and the expected output from each case. The test cases should be chosen carefully. The *code-coverage* approach designs test cases to ensure that each statement in the program is executed. The *data-coverage* approach designs test cases to ensure that the limits of the allowable data are covered. Often testing is a combination of code and data coverage.

Implementing a test plan means that you run each of the test cases described in the test plan and record the results. If the results are not as expected, you must go back to your design and find and correct the error(s). The process stops when each of the test cases gives the expected results. Note that an implemented test plan gives you a measure of confidence that your program is correct; however, all you know for sure is that your program works correctly on your test cases. Therefore, the quality of your test cases is extremely important.

An example of a test plan for the code fragment that tests temperatures is shown here. We assume that the fragment is embedded in a program that reads in a data value that represents a temperature.

Reason for Test Case	Input	Expected Output	Observed Output
Test first end point	32	Today is a cold day.	
Test second end point	85	Today is a nice day.	
Test value below first end point	31	Today is a cold day.	

Test value between end points	45	Today is a nice day.
Test value above second end point	86	Today is a hot day.
Test negative value	-10	Today is a cold day.

To implement this test plan, the program is run six times, once for each test case. The results are written in the Observed Output column.

Warning

The assignment operator (=) and the equality test operator (==) can easily be miskeyed one for the other. What happens if this occurs? Unfortunately, the program does not crash; it continues to execute but probably gives incorrect results. Look at the following two statements.

```
aValue == aValue + 1;      // aValue = aValue + 1 is meant
if (value1 = value2)       // if (value1 == value2) is meant
```

The first statement returns `false`: `aValue` can never be equal to `aValue + 1`. The semicolon ends the statement, so nothing happens to the value returned (`aValue + 1`) and execution continues with the next statement. `aValue` has not been changed. In the second case, although we think of `value1` = `value2` as being an assignment statement, it is technically just an expression that does two things: It returns the value of the expression on the right of the equal sign, and it stores this value in the place on the left. Here, the value returned is the content of `value2`.

The moral of this story is to be very careful when you key your program. A simple keying error can cause logic errors that the compiler does not catch and that are very difficult for the user to find. Great care and a good test plan are essential to Java programming.

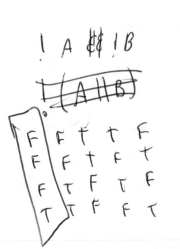

Laboratory 4: Prelab Assignment

Name _Jerry Reed_   Date _____

Section _____

Exercise 1: Examine the following pairs of expressions and determine if they are equivalent. Put a T in the Result column if they are the same and an F if they are not.

Expression 1	Expression 2	Result
(A == B)	A != B	T
! ((A == B) || (A == C))	(A != B) && (A != C)	T
! ((A == B) && (C > D))	(A != B) || (C <= D)	T

$$A != B \mid\mid C <= D$$

Exercise 2: Examine the following pairs of expressions and determine if they are logically equivalent. Put a T in the Result column if they are the same and an F if they are not.

Expression 1	Expression 2	Result
!A && B	B && !A	T
!A || B	B || !A	T
!(A && B)	A || B	F
A && B || C	A && (B || C)	F
(A && B || C)	!(A || B && C)	F

Exercise 3: Examine the following code segments and determine the result of the requested expression.

Code Segment		Returns
s1 = "Hello";		
s2 = "hello";		hello
s1.equals(s2);		

X Y
T Tt
F T F
F F T
F F F

T
T
T
F

A && B \|\| C

T
T
T
F
F
F

```
s1 = "Hello";
s2 = "hello";
toUpperCase(s1).equals(toUpperCase(s2))
```

Hello

```
s1 = "Hello";
s2 = "hello";
s1 == s3
s1 = "Good By";
s2 = "GoodBy";
s1.compareTo(s2)
s2.compareTo(s1)
s1.compareTo("Good By")
```

Hello

GoodBy

GoodBy

Good By

Lesson 4–1: Check Prelab Exercises

Name _____ Date _____

Section _____

Exercise 1: The answers are T, T, and T.

Exercise 2: The answers are T, T, F, F, and F.

Exercise 3: The answers are false, true, false, -1, +1, and 0.

Lesson 4-2: Boolean Expressions

Name _____   Date _____

Section _____

Use program Shell for Exercises 1, 2, and 3.

```
// Program Shell prints appropriate messages on System.out
//  based on a grade read from the keyboard
import java.io.*;      — import keyboard

public class Shell
{
  public static void main(String[] args)     throws IoException
  {
    int grade;   — makes it
    BufferedReader inData;
    inData =
      newBufferedReader(newInputStreamReader(System.in));

    System.out.println("Key in an integer grade. ");
    grade = Integer.parseInt(inData.readLine());
    if                                              → take what Typed till enter
    // Enter rest of the program beginning here.



  }
}
```

Name to keyboard

makes char(s) from keyboard

Exercise 1: When completed, program Shell reads an integer value and writes an appropriate message on System.out. Complete the *if* statement so that "Congratulations!" is written if the numeric grade is greater than or equal to 80. Run the program five times entering the following values for grade: 60, 100, 80, 81, and 79.

"Congratulations!" is printed _____ time(s) in the five runs.

Exercise 2: Change the Boolean expression in Exercise 1 so that "Try harder" is printed if the numeric grade is less than 70. Run the program with the same data listed for Exercise 1.

"Try harder" is printed _____ time(s) in the five runs.

Exercise 3: Change the Boolean expression so that "Average" is printed if the numeric grade is less than 80 but greater than 70. Run the program with the same data listed for Exercise 1.

"Average" is printed_____ time(s) in the five runs.

Lesson 4-3: if Statements

Name _____ Date _____

Section _____

Use program `Shell2` for the exercises in this lesson. This program prompts for and reads an integer value, and then prints a message based on this value.

```
// Program Shell2 prints appropriate messages based on a
//   pressure reading input from the keyboard

import java.io.*;

public class Shell
{
  public static void main(String[] args)
  {
    int pressure;
    BufferedReader inData;
    inData =
      new BufferedReader(new InputStreamReader(System.in));

    // Enter rest of the program beginning here.


  }
}
```

Exercise 1: Insert a statement that reads in the pressure reading and writes the following warning to the screen if the pressure reading is greater than 100.

"Warning!! Pressure reading above danger limit."

Run your program eight times using the following values as input: 6, 76, 80, 99, 0, 100, 110, 199

"Warning!! Pressure reading above danger limit." is printed _____ times.

If your answer is 2, your *if* statement is correct. If your answer is 3, the relational operator on your expression is incorrect. It should be greater than, not greater than or equal to. Rerun your corrected program.

Exercise 2: Insert a statement in program `Shell2` that writes the following message if the pressure reading is lower than 100 but greater than 6.

"Everything seems normal."

Run your program eight times using the same data that you used in Exercise 1.

"Everything seems normal" is printed _____ times.

Lesson 4-4: if-else Statements

Name _____ Date _____

Section _____

Exercise 1: Take program Shell2 in Lesson 4-3 and change it so that it prints the message in both Lesson 4-3, Exercise 1, and Lesson 4-3, Exercise 2. Run the program with the data set for Lesson 4-3, Exercise 1.

"Warning!! Pressure reading above danger limit." is printed _____ times.

"Everything seems normal" is printed _____ times.

Use program Shell3 for Exercises 2, 3, and 4.

```java
// Program Shell3 calculates a person's percentage of
//   calories from fat and prints an appropriate message

import java.io.*;
public class Shell3
{

  public static void main(String[] args)
  {
    BufferedReader inData;
    inData =
      new BufferedReader(new InputStreamReader(System.in));

    String foodItem;
    int gramsOfFat;
    int calories;
    double fatCalPercent;

    System.out.println("Enter name of food item.");
    // Input name of food item.

    System.out.println("Enter number of calories.");
    // Input number of calories

    System.out.println("Enter grams of fat.");
    // Input grams of fat

    // Rest of program

  }
}
```

Exercise 2: The American Heart Association recommends that no more than 30 percent of a person's daily calories come from fat. Each gram of fat is nine calories. Given the grams of fat and the number of calories in an item, we can calculate the percentage of calories that comes from fat. Add statements to program She113 to input the name of the item (foodItem), the number of calories (calories), and grams of fat (gramsOfFat) and write the item and the percentage of calories that come from fat (fatCalPercent) on System.out. Run your program four times with the following data:

Item	Grams of Fat	Calories	Percent from Fat
Tuna	1	60	16 %
Spaetzle	2	170	10 %
V8 Juice	0	36	0 %
Corned Beef	7	200	31 %

Exercise 3: Add a statement to program She113 from Exercise 2 that prints one of the following two messages depending on the percentage of calories from fat (value of fatCalPercent).

"This item is Heart Healthy!"
"This item is NOT Heart Healthy!!"

Run your program using the data in Exercise 2.

Which of the items are heart healthy?

Exercise 4: Your test should look like one of the following where fatCalOK is a boolean variable:

```
fatCalOK = fatCalPercent <= 0.30;
if (fatCalOK)

if (fatCalPercent <= 0.30)

fatCalOK = fatCalPercent <= 0.30;
if (fatCalOK == true)

if ((fatCalPercent <= 0.30) == true)
```

Circle the one that you used in your program. If you used the first or the second, you understand Boolean expressions and *if* statements. If you used one of the others, you are correct, but you have redundant code. A Boolean variable contains one of the constants true or false, and a Boolean expression returns true or false. You do not need to compare the Boolean variable or expression with the value true.

Lesson 4–5: Nested Logic

Name _____ Date _____

Section _____

Use the following shell for the exercises in this lesson.

```
// Program Shell4 inputs a temperature and prints an
//  appropriate message

import java.io.*;
public class Shell4
{
  public static void main(String[] args)
  {
    int temperature;
    BufferedReader inData;
    inData =
      new BufferedReader(new InputStreamReader(System.in));

    System.out.println("Enter temperature and pressreturn.");
    temperature = Integer.parseInt(inData.readLine());

    // Rest of program

  }
}
```

Exercise 1: Add five *if* statements to program `Shell4` so that one of the following messages is printed based on the value of `temperature`.

Temperature	Message
> 90	"Visit a neighbor."
<= 90, > 80	"Turn on air conditioning."
<= 80, > 70	"Do nothing."
<= 70, >66	"Turn on heat."
<= 66	"Visit a neighbor."

Run your program as many times as it takes to write each message exactly once. What data values did you use?

Exercise 2: Rewrite the program in Exercise 1 using nested logic (i.e., *if-else* where the *else* branch is an *if* statement). Rerun the program with the same data. Did you get the same answers? Explain.

Exercise 3: Complete program `HiScore` so that it reads three test scores from the window, then labels and prints the largest of the three on `System.out`.

```java
// Program HiScore reads and prints three test scores.
//   The largest value of the three is printed with an
//   appropriate message
// Assumption:  The scores are unique

import java.io.*;

public class HiScore
{
  public static void main(String[] args)
  {
    BufferedReader inData;
    inData =
      new BufferedReader(new InputStreamReader(System.in));

    int score1;
    int score2;
    int score3;

    // Prompt for and read in scores
    System.out.println("Enter the score for test one.");
    score1 = Integer.parseInt(inData.readLine());
    System.out.println("Enter the score for test two.");
    score2 = Integer.parseInt(inData.readLine());
    System.out.println("Enter the score for test three.");
    score3 = Integer.parseInt(inData.readLine());

    // Fill in the rest of the program
  }
}
```

Fill in the missing statement(s) in program `HiScore` so that the largest of the three input values (scores) is printed and labeled as the highest test score. You may use a nested *if* statement or a series of *if* statements. For example, if `test2Score` with a value of 98 is the largest, your output might look as follows:

```
The value for test 2 is the highest; it is 98.
```

Your message may be different, but it must include the largest value and which test had that value. Run your program three times using the three sets of input values listed below.

Input values   *What is printed*

100   80   70   _____

 70   80 100   _____

 80 100   60   _____

Lesson 4-6: Test Plan

Name _____ Date _____

Section _____

Exercise 1: Design a test plan for program `HiScore` in Lesson 4-5. (*Hint:* There should be at least six test cases.)

Reason for Test Case	Input Values	Expected Output	Observed Output

Exercise 2: Implement the test plan designed in Exercise 1. You may show the results in the chart in Exercise 1.

Postlab Activities

Exercise 1: Your history instructor gives three tests worth 60 points each. You can drop one of the first two grades. The final grade is the sum of the best of the first two grades and the third grade. Given three test grades, write a program that calculates the final letter grade using the following cut-off points.

>= 90	A
< 90, >= 80	B
< 80, >= 70	C
< 70, >= 60	D
< 60	F

Your program should prompt for and read the grades from the screen; write your output to `System.out`.

Exercise 2: Write a program to determine if the digits in a three-digit number are all odd, all even, or mixed odd and even. Your program should prompt the user to input a three-digit number. If the digits in the number are all odd, write "This number contains all odd digits." If the digits are all even, write "This number contains all even digits." If the number contains both odd and even digits, write "This number contains both odd and even digits." Use integer division and modulus to access the digits in the number.

Exercise 3: The world outside of the United States has switched to Celsius. You are going to travel in England, where the temperature is given in Celsius. A friend said that a quick approximation of the Fahrenheit equivalent of a Celsius number is to take the number, double it, and add 32. Write a program that takes as input a temperature in Celsius and calculates both the approximated Fahrenheit equivalent and the actual Fahrenheit equivalent. Write out all three values. If the approximation and the actual value are within two degrees, write out "Close enough." If they are not within two degrees, write out "Will not do."

Exercise 4: In Laboratory 3, Postlab Exercise 5, you wrote a program that calculated the body mass index (BMI). Enhance that program so that it prints on the screen an interpretation of the BMI. Use the following scale.

BMI	Interpretation
Under 16	Emaciated
16 – 19	Underweight
20 – 24	Normal
26 – 30	Overweight
Over 30	Obese

Homework

File I/O and Looping

- ■ To be able to construct input and output statements that take their input from a file and send their output to a file.

- ■ To be able to modify a program containing a *while* statement.

- ■ To be able to construct a count-controlled loop to implement a specified task.

- ■ To be able to construct an event-controlled loop to implement a specified task.

- ■ To be able to construct a loop nested within another loop.

- ■ To be able to test the state of an I/O stream.

- ■ To be able to answer questions about a loop that you have implemented.

Laboratory 5: Assignment Cover Sheet

Name _____ Date _____

Section _____

Fill in the following table showing which exercises have been assigned for each lesson and check what you are to submit: (1) lab sheets, (2) listings of output files, and/or (3) listings of code. Your instructor or teaching assistant (TA) can use the Completed column for grading purposes.

Activities	Assigned: Check or list exercise numbers	Submit (1) (2) (3)			Completed
Prelab					
Review					
Prelab Assignment					
Inlab					
Lesson 5-1: Check Prelab Exercises					
Lesson 5-2: Input and Output with Files					
Lesson 5-3: Count-Controlled Loops					
Lesson 5-4: Event-Controlled Loops					
Lesson 5-5: Nested Logic					
Lesson 5-6: Debugging					
Postlab					

Prelab Activities

Review

The sample program in Laboratory 1 used file input and `System.out` for output. In subsequent chapters, we have used interactive input based in `System.in`. If you want to prepare input data ahead, you can store the data in a file and direct the program to read its input from a file. If you want to save output data to use later, you may direct the program to write data to a file. In this chapter, we examine file input and the looping construct that allows the program to continue reading data values until they have all been read.

Input Files

Let's look at the program from Laboratory 1 and go through it carefully. By now, the only unfamiliar constructs are those examined in this chapter: files and loops.

```java
import java.io.*;    // Access file classes
public class RainFall
{
  // Declare dataFile for input
  private static BufferedReader dataFile;

  static double getInches(BufferedReader dataFile,
    int numberDays) throws IOException
  // Reads and returns the total inches of rain
  {
    double total = 0.0;
    double inches;
    int days = 1;
    while (days <= numberDays)
    {
      inches =
        Double.parseDouble(dataFile.readLine());
      total = total + inches;
      days++;
    }
    return total;
  }

  public static void main(String[] args) throws IOException
  // Main is where execution starts.  It opens the data file,
  //   reads the number of days of rain to be totaled, calls an
  //   auxiliary method to read and sum the rainfall, and
  //   prints the average rainfall on the screen
  {
    double totalRain;
    int numDays;
    double average;
    // Instantiate and open the data file.
    dataFile = new BufferedReader(
      new FileReader("rainFile.in"));
```

Keyboard

```
      // Input the number of days
      numDays = Integer.ParseInt(dataFile.readLine()).intValue();

      totalRain = getInches(dataFile, numDays);

      if (numDays == 0)
        System.out.println("Average cannot be computed "
            + "for 0 days.");
      else
      {
        average = totalRain / numDays;
        System.out.println("The average rainfall over " +
          numDays + " days is " + average);
      }
      dataFile.close();
  }
}
```

The first statement imports the classes that we need in order to read from a file. They are in package java.io. The fifth line declares an object of class BufferedReader, a class that describes input files. The next section defines a method getInches. This method is an *auxiliary* or *helper* method. It is an action that is given a name and then invoked from with method main. Helper methods allow us to encapsulate an action and then execute the action from somewhere else in the code.

The fourth line within main instantiates the data file. Let's look at it piece by piece.

```
dataFile = new BufferedReader(new FileReader("rainFile.in"));
```

dataFile, the file variable, is instantiated by a call to its class constructor: So far so good. However, the parameter to the constructor is a constructor for another class named FileReader, which in turn takes a string as a parameter. It looks more complex than it really is. BufferedReader is a class derived from FileReader, and its constructor takes an instance of its base class as a parameter. The string that is a parameter to the FileReader constructor is the name by which the file is known on the disk.

The next statement should look very familiar.

```
numDays = Integer.parseInt(dataFile.readLine());
```

We have used a similar statement to get a string value from a window and convert it to an integer value and store it in an integer variable. That's exactly what this statement does, except that it gets its value from a file rather than a window. Which file? rainFile.in. The next statement that contains a reference to dataFile is this one:

```
totalRain = getInches(dataFile, numDays);
```

Here dataFile is being passed as a parameter to method getInches, where a floating-point value is read from the file using the following statement.

```
inches = Double.parseDouble(dataFile.readLine());
```

The last statement that involves the file is

```
dataFile.close();
```

which closes the file.

Here is a list of the methods in class `BufferedReader` and what they do.

Method	Description
`skip(long n)`	Skips n characters; an error occurs if there are not n characters before the end of file.
`close()`	Breaks the correspondence between the file variable and the file on disk.
`readLine()`	Returns a string made up of a line (end of line is read but not returned); returns `null`, a special Java value that doesn't correspond to any valid data value, if there is no more data.

Methods `skip` and `close` are inherited from `FileReader`.

This program demonstrates all the steps necessary in declaring and using a data file: import the file classes, declare a file variable, instantiate the file object, read values from the file, and close the file.

There is one more point concerning input files: Reading from a file can generate an error. In Laboratory 9, we explain how to handle such errors, but for now we handle them by adding a clause to the main method: `throws IOException`. This clause tells the system that `IOExceptions` (errors) are not being handled within this application.

Output Files

The program in Chapter 1 used `System.out` for output rather than a file. The class that is a pattern for an output file is `PrintWriter`, a class derived from `FileWriter`. We instantiate an output file like we do an input file.

```
PrintWriter outFile;
outFile = new PrintWriter(new FileWriter("data.out"));
```

An anonymous object of class `FileWriter` is created and sent as a parameter to the constructor for a `PrintWriter` object. The string parameter is the name of the file on the disk when the application finishes executing. The methods in class `PrintWriter` are `print`, `println`, and `close`. Methods `print` and `println` behave exactly as the `print` and `println` methods associated with `System.out` behave.

Creating a Data File

If you are using an integrated environment, such as Borland's Turbo Java, Microsoft's Visual J++, or Metrowerk's CodeWarrior, an editor is provided for you in which to write your program. You may use this same editor to create a data file. That is, instead of writing a Java program, you key in the data you want the program to read.

If you are using a general-purpose word processor to create your programs, such as Word or WordPerfect, you may use this same editor to create your data files. However, you need to save both your programs and your data files in text mode. General-purpose word processors have formatting information at the beginning of the file that you cannot see on the screen. This information must be removed from the file before the compiler can compile the program or the program can read data correctly. If the program file has formatting information, the compiler cannot compile the program and alerts you that there is a problem. If the data file has formatting information, you simply get the wrong answer.

Looping

In Laboratory 4, we looked at Boolean expressions and how they can be used in the *if* statement to make a choice. In this chapter, we examine how Boolean expressions can be used in a *while* statement to make the program repeat a statement or group of statements. Such repetitions are called *loops*.

while Statement

The *if* statement allows the program to skip the execution of a statement or choose between one of two statements to be executed based on the value of a Boolean expression. In contrast, the *while* statement allows a program to continue executing a statement as long as the value of a Boolean expression is true. When the Boolean expression becomes false, execution of the program continues with the statement immediately following the *while* statement. Look at the following code fragment.

```
sum = 0;
count = 1;
while (count <= 10)
{
  value = Integer.parseInt(dataFile.readLine());
  sum = sum + value;
  count++;
}
outFile.println("The sum of the 10 numbers is " + sum);
```

The variables `sum` and `count` are assigned the values 0 and 1, respectively. The Boolean expression (`count <= 10`) is evaluated. The value in `count` is less than or equal to 10, so the expression is `true` and the block (compound statement) associated with the *while* statement is executed. A number is extracted from file `dataFile` and added to `sum`. The value in `count` is incremented by 1.

At this point, the logical order of the program diverges from the physical order. The *while* expression is evaluated again. Because the value stored in `count` is still less than or equal to 10, the compound statement associated with the *while* is executed again. This process continues until `count` contains the value 11. At that time, the expression is no longer `true`, the body of the *while* statement is not executed again, and execution continues with the statement immediately following the *while* statement that sends the labeled answer to the file.

Types of Loops

There are two basic types of loops: count-controlled and event-controlled. A *count-controlled loop* is one that is executed a certain number of times. The expression that controls the loop becomes false when the loop has executed the prescribed number of times. An *event-controlled loop* is one whose execution is controlled by the occurrence of an event within the loop itself. The previous example is a count-controlled loop that executes 10 times. Let's look at an example of an event-controlled loop that reads and sums values from a file until a negative value is encountered.

```
sum = 0;
value = Integer.parseInt(dataFile.readLine());

// Set moreData to true if the first data item is not
//  negative; false otherwise.
moreData = value >= 0;

while (moreData)
{
  sum = sum + value;
  value = Integer.parseInt(dataFile.readLine());
  moreData = value >= 0;   // Reset moreData
}
outFile.println("The sum of the values prior to "
  + "a negative value is " + sum);
```

sum is set to zero and the first data item (`value`) is read outside of the loop. `value` is compared to zero and the result is stored in `moreData`. If the first data item is less than zero, `moreData` is `false`, and the body of the loop is not executed. If the first data item is greater than or equal to zero, `moreData` is `true`, and the body of the loop is entered. `value` is added to `sum`, and the next data item is read. This new data item is compared to zero, and `moreData` is reset. The expression is tested again. This process continues until a value of less than zero is read and `moreData` becomes `false`. When this happens, the body of the *while* is not executed again, and the sum of the nonnegative numbers is sent to the output stream.

Reading the first value outside of the body of the loop is called a *priming read*. When a priming read is used before a loop, the input values are processed at the beginning of the loop body and a subsequent read occurs at the end of the loop body.

Notice the difference between these two loops. The first reads ten values and sums them; the second reads and sums values until a negative number is read. The first is count-controlled; the second is event-controlled. The second loop is called a sentinel-controlled loop because reading a sentinel (a negative number) is the event that controls it.

EOF Loops

We can read and process data values until all of the data has been read. When the last data value has been read, the file is at the end of the file (called EOF). The file is fine until another data value is requested. At that point, `readLine` returns `null`. If we are going to test for `null`, we must do so before the string is converted to a numeric value. Therefore, we must reorganize our input slightly as shown on the next page.

```
sum = 0;
inputString = dataFile.readLine();
while (inputString != null)
{
  value = Integer.parseInt(inputString);
  sum = sum + value;
  inputString = dataFile.readLine();
}
```

Because readLine does not return null until we try to access a value when the file is at EOF, we must use a priming read as we did in the previous example. If there is a value, readLine returns a valid string and the body of the loop is entered where the string is converted and added to sum and a new string is read. After the last value has been processed, the attempt to read one more value returns null. When the *while* expression is tested the last time, inputString is null and the loop is not repeated.

Proper Loop Operation

For obvious reasons, the *while* statement is called a loop or looping statement. The statement that is being executed within the loop is called the *body* of the loop.

There are three basic steps that must be done for a loop to operate properly.

1. The variables in the expression (the counter or event) must be set (initialized) before the *while* statement is executed the first time.
2. The expression must test the status of the counter or event correctly so that the body of the loop executes when it is supposed to and terminates at the proper time.
3. The counter or the status of the event must be updated within the loop. If the counter or the status of the event is not updated, the loop never stops executing. This situation is called an *infinite loop*.

Nested Loops

The body of the loop can contain any type of statement including another *while* statement. The following program counts the number of blanks on each line in a file. We use readLine to input a line from the file, indexOf to find the position of the first blank, and substring to replace the string with all the characters up to and including the blank removed. Let's enclose this nested loop within a complete application to show all the pieces we have been talking about in this chapter.

```
// Application IOLoop counts the number of blanks per line
//   and the number of lines in a file
import java.io.*;
public class IOLoop
{
  public static BufferedReader inFile;
  public static PrintWriter outFile;

  public static void main(String[] args) throws IOException
  {
    int lineCount = 0;
    int blankCount;
    int index;
```

```
   String inputString;
   inFile = new BufferedReader(new FileReader("history.dat"));
   outFile = new PrintWriter(new FileWriter("data.out"));
   inputString = inFile.readLine();
   while (inputString != null)
   {
     lineCount++;
     blankCount = 0;
     index = inputString.indexOf(' ');
     while (index != -1)
     {
       blankCount++;
       if (inputString.length() != 1)
       {
         inputString = inputString.substring(index+1,
           inputString.length());
         index = inputString.indexOf(' ');
       }
       else index = -1;
     }
     outFile.println("Line " + lineCount + " contains "
       + blankCount + " blanks.");
     inputString = inFile.readLine();
   }
   outFile.close();
   inFile.close();
 }
}
```

Laboratory 5: Prelab Assignment

Name _____   Date _____

Section _____

Examine the following application and answer the questions in Exercises 1 through 4.

```
import java.io.*;
public class IOLoop2
{
  public static BufferedReader inFile;
  public static PrintWriter outFile;
  public static void main(String[] args)throws IOException
  {
    int numberCount = 0;
    int value;
    String inputString;
    inFile = new BufferedReader(new FileReader("data.in"));
    outFile = new PrintWriter(new FileWriter("data2.out"));
    inputString = inFile.readLine();
    while (inputString != null)
    {
      outFile.print(inputString);
      inputString = inFile.readLine();
      value = Integer.parseInt(inputString);
      outFile.println("" + value);
      numberCount++;
      inputString = inFile.readLine();
    }
    outFile.println("There are" + numberCount
      + " data values in the file.");
    outFile.close();
    inFile.close();
  }
}
```

File `data.in` contains the following lines.

```
The first data value is
1066
The second data value is
1492
The third data value is
1939
The fourth data value is
1944
The fifth data value is
2000
```

Exercise 1: Show what is written on `outFile`.

Exercise 2: There is an implicit assumption in this program. What is it?

Exercise 3: What happens if the number of lines of data is odd?

Exercise 4: Why does this application have a priming read?

Lesson 5–1: Check Prelab Exercises

Name _____ Date _____

Section _____

Exercise 1: Run program `IOLoop2` and check your answer. Did one of the answers surprise you? Can you explain it?

Exercise 2: The number of lines of code is even: a line of text and a line with a data value.

Exercise 3: A `NumberFormatException` is thrown and the program halts.

Exercise 4: The loop is an EOF loop. The first line of data must be read in and then tested against `null`.

Lesson 5–2: Input and Output with Files

Name _____ Date _____

Section _____

Exercises 1 through 4 use program shell `ReadData`.

```java
import java.io.*;
public class ReadData
{
  /* TO BE FILLED IN: Exercise 1 */
  public static void main(String[] args) throws IOException
  {
    /* TO BE FILLED IN: Exercise 2 */
    int count = 0;
    int value;
    int sum = 0;
    while (count < 10)
    {
      value = /* TO BE FILLED IN: Exercise 3 */
      sum = sum + value;
      count++;
    }
    /* TO BE FILLED IN: Exercise 4 */
  }
}
```

Exercise 1: Declare an input file `firstIn` and an output file `firstOut`.

Exercise 2: Instantiate your files. The input data is on file `data`; the output file should go on file `outData` on the disk.

Exercise 3: Read a value and convert it to an integer.

Exercise 4: Write a statement that writes the sum of the values on the output file.

Exercise 5: Run your program and show what is written on file `outData`.

Lesson 5–3: Count–Controlled Loops

Name _____   Date _____

Section _____

Exercise 1: Class `ReadData` contained a count-controlled loop with the loop counter going from 0 to 9. Rewrite the loop so that it goes from 1 to 10. Compile and run the program. What is written on the output file?

Exercise 2: Change class `ReadData` so that the number of data values is a variable rather than a literal. The number of data values is the first value on the file. Run your program using file `data1`. What is written on the output file?

Exercise 3: What happens if there are more values on the file than are specified by the first value?

Exercise 4: What happens if there are fewer values on the file than are specified by the first value?

Lesson 5-4: Event-Controlled Loops

Name _____ Date _____

Section _____

Use application `OddEven` for Exercises 1 through 3.

```java
import java.io.*;
public class OddEven
{
  public static BufferedReader inFile;
  public static PrintWriter outFile;
  public static void main(String[] args) throws IOException
  {
    float value;
    String inputString;
    int oddCount = 0;
    int evenCount = 0;
    inFile = new BufferedReader(new FileReader("data3.in"));
    outFile = new PrintWriter(new FileWriter("data3.out"));
    inputString = inFile.readLine();
    value = Float.parseFloat(inputString);
    while (/* TO BE FILLED IN: Exercise 1 */)
    {
      /* TO BE FILLED IN: Exercise 2 */
    }
    /* TO BE FILLED IN: Exercise 3 */
    outFile.close();
    inFile.close();
  }
}
```

Exercise 1: Write the *while* expression that returns true if the first data value is not zero.

Exercise 2: Write the loop body that counts the number of odd and even values in file `inFile`.

Exercise 3: Write the output statement that writes the number of odd and even values on file `outFile`. Compile and run your program. What is written on file `data3.out`?

Lesson 5-5: Nested Logic

Name _____ Date _____

Section _____

Exercise 1: Run program IOLoop. What was written on file data.out?

Exercise 2: The number of blanks comes close to estimating the number of words in a text file. Look carefully at the code and the data file. Alter the code so that the count reflects the number of words in the file. Compile and rerun the program. Now what is written on file data.out?

Lesson 5–6: Debugging

Name _____ Date _____

Section _____

Exercise 1: Program SumNums reads and counts nonnegative integers until there are no more data values. You run the program using file SumNums.D1, and the program can't find the file. You know that there are nine values on the file and that seven of them are nonnegative. Locate the bug and describe it.

Exercise 2: The program now runs, but it gives the wrong answer. Locate and describe this bug.

Exercise 3: The answer is different but still wrong! Keep looking. Describe the error.

Postlab Activities

Exercise 1: Write a program to print a triangle composed of a symbol. The number of lines in the triangle and the symbol should be entered as input from a window. For example, if the input values are 7 and #, the output is as follows:

```
      #
     ###
    #####
   #######
  #########
 ###########
#############
```

In your program documentation, describe the loop(s) used as count-controlled or event-controlled.

Exercise 2: File `History.d1` contains a brief history of computing. There are no indentations in this file. Write a program to read this file, inserting five blank spaces at the beginning of each paragraph. You can recognize a paragraph because a blank line appears before the first line of each paragraph. Write the changed file on `History.d2`. In your program documentation, describe the loop(s) used as count-controlled or event-controlled.

Exercise 3: As a child, did you ever play the game "One potato, two potato, . . ." to determine who would be "it"? The complete rhyme is given below:

One potato, two potato, three potato, four;
Five potato, six potato, seven potato, more.
O U T spells "out you go."

A child is pointed to during each phrase. There are four phrases each in lines 1 and 2 and seven phrases in line 3, so the last child pointed to is the 15th one. If there are fewer than 15 children, you go around the circle again. The child pointed to when the word *go* is said is "out." The game begins again with the remaining children, starting again with the first child. The last child remaining is "it."

Simulate this game in a computer program. The input is the number of children; the output is which child is "it."

Exercise 4: Modify the game in Exercise 4 so that rather than beginning again with child number 1, you start again with the child following the last one out.

Exercise 5: In Laboratory 4, Postlab Exercise 3, you were asked to determine the accuracy of an approximation of a translation of a temperature from Celsius to Fahrenheit. The Fahrenheit approximation is the Celsius number doubled plus 32. Write a program that creates a table with three columns. The first column contains temperatures in Celsius, the second contains the Fahrenheit approximation, and the third contains the actual Fahrenheit equivalent. Run your program using at least 10 data values. Examine your table and write a paragraph discussing the accuracy of the approximation.

Exercise 6: There is a temperature for which Fahrenheit and Celsius are the same. This value can be determined both algebraically and experimentally. Solve the problem algebraically first and then write a program that determines if a solution exists by experimentation.

Review of Classes and Methods, and Software Design Strategies

- To be able to declare and instantiate a new class.

- To be able to distinguish between primitive parameters and reference parameters.

- To be able to implement class constructors.

- To be able to implement other class methods.

- To be able to create a Java package.

- To be able to apply the object-oriented strategy to solve a simple problem.

- To be able to apply the functional decomposition strategy to solve a simple problem.

Laboratory 6: Assignment Cover Sheet

Name _____ Date _____

Section _____

Fill in the following table showing which exercises have been assigned for each lesson and check what you are to submit: (1) lab sheets, (2) listings of output files, and/or (3) listings of code. Your instructor or teaching assistant (TA) can use the Completed column for grading purposes.

Activities	Assigned: Check or list exercise numbers	Submit (1) (2) (3)			Completed
Prelab					
Review					
Prelab Assignment					
Inlab					
Lesson 6-1: Check Prelab Exercises					
Lesson 6-2: Classes					
Lesson 6-3: Constructors					
Lesson 6-4: Methods and Parameters					
Lesson 6-5: Program Design					
Lesson 6-6: Debugging					
Postlab					

Prelab Activities

Review

In previous laboratories, we have covered the syntax and semantics of Java classes and methods. In this laboratory, we review these topics and turn our attention to design strategies.

Classes

The `class` is a Java language feature that encourages good programming style by allowing the user to encapsulate both data and actions into a single object.

```
public class Money
{
  private long dollars;
  private long cents;

  public void  initialize(long newDollars, long newCents);
  // Initializes dollars and cents
  {
    dollars = newDollars;
    cents = newCents;
  }

  public long  dollarsAre()
  // Returns dollars
  {
    return dollars;
  }

  public long  centsAre()
  // Returns cents
  {
    return cents;
  }
}
...
Money money;
```

`Money` is a `class`; it is a pattern for a structure. This pattern has two data fields (member variables), `dollars` and `cents`, and three actions (methods), `initialize`, `dollarsAre`, and `centsAre`. The word `public` modifying a method means that the method is accessible to anyone using the class (defining a variable of the class). The data members defined with the `private` modifier are accessible only to the class's methods. Member variables and methods defined as `public` form the interface between the class and its *clients*. A client is any software that declares variables of the class.

The object that `money` refers to is an instance of the `class Money`; it is called a *class instance* or *class object*, often shortened to *object*. `money` has two member variables and three methods. To apply a class instance's methods, you append the method name to the object separated by a period. For example, the following code segment instructs `money` to apply its methods `initialize`, `dollarsAre`, and `centsAre` to itself.

```
money.initialize(56, 23);
System.out.println("" + money.dollarsAre());
System.out.println("" + money.centsAre());
```

When the statement

```
money.initialize(56, 23);
```

is executed, 56 is stored in `money.dollars` and 23 is stored in `money.cents`. Because `initialize` is an action defined within class `Money`, any invocation of `initialize` is applied to a specific instance of `Money`, in this case an object referred to by the variable `money`. The variable identifiers used in the body of the definition of `initialize` refer to those of the instance to which it is applied.

The following statement prints the data fields of `money`.

```
System.out.println("$" + money.dollarsAre()
     + "."  + money.centsAre());
```

Class Constructors

Our class `Money` is incomplete because we have not defined a constructor for the class. Recall that a class is a reference type, and therefore must be instantiated using a constructor. A class constructor is a method with the same name as the class.

```
public  Money()                        // Default constructor
// Sets dollars and cents to 0
{
    dollars = 0;
    cents   = 0;
}

public Money(long initDollars, long initCents)
// Parameterized constructor that sets dollars and cents
{
  dollars = initDollars;
  cents   = initCents;
}

Money   money = new Money();
Money   myMoney = new Money(5000, 98);
```

There are two constructors: one with no parameters, called the default constructor, and one with two parameters. They look a little strange because there is no type identifier or `void` before them. Constructors are invoked differently than other methods as well. A class constructor is invoked when a class instance is instantiated. In this example, `money` is instantiated using the default class constructor (the one with no parameters), and `myMoney` is instantiated using 5000 in `dollars` and 98 in `cents`.

Notice that class constructors do not make method `initialize` unnecessary. If you want to reinitialize a class object after it has been instantiated, you must use method `initialize`. When you combine a variable or a collection of variables with the operations that create and manipulate them, you have an *abstract data type*.

More about Methods and Parameters

Methods `centsAre` and `dollarsAre` are value-returning methods. The `long` in the headings of the methods specifies the type of the values being returned. Value-returning methods are used in expressions as shown in the example. Method `initialize` is a void method as evidenced by the keyword `void` in its heading. Void methods do not return values. They are named actions that are used as statements in the program.

Methods `centsAre` and `dollarsAre` do not have any parameters; that is, the parentheses beside the method heading are empty. Method `initialize` has two parameters. The first, `newDollars`, is stored into `dollars`; the second, `newCents`, is stored into `cents`. Which `dollars` and `cents`? The `dollars` and `cents` data fields of the object to which `initialize` is applied: `money` in the example in the previous section.

Parameters are the names of the variables in the heading of a method; arguments are the variables in a method call. The variables or expressions in a method call are substituted for the parameters within the body of the method when it is executed. The first argument is substituted for the first parameter; the second argument is substituted for the second parameter, and so on. The arguments and parameters must be of the same type or class. Arguments and parameters are the way that a client passes information to a class's methods.

All arguments in Java are passed by value. This means that a copy of the argument is sent to the method, not the argument itself. If the parameter is a primitive type, the argument cannot be changed because the method has a copy, not the argument itself. If a parameter is a reference type, the address of the argument is passed to the method. This address cannot be changed, but the *contents* of that address could be changed. However, this is poor programming style. If a class instance needs to be changed, an instance method should be defined within the class rather than defining a method that takes the instance as a parameter.

Binary Operations

When a binary operation is defined within a class, one of the operands is passed as a parameter and the other is the class instance to which the method is applied. For example, let's assume that a binary operation, `add`, has been included as a method in `Money`. Here is its definition.

```
public Money  add(Money  value)
// Returns sum of object plus value.
{
  Money  result = new Money();
  result.cents = cents + value.cents;
  result.dollars = dollars + value.dollars;
  return result;
}
```

Given the following statement,

```
result = money.add(value);
```

cents and dollars in the code of method add refer to those members in the class object to which add has been applied—that is, to money.cents and money.dollars. The class object to which a method is applied is called this. Thus we say that cents and dollars without a variable appended refer to self or this.

Lifetime of Data

There are three categories of data associated with a class: class data, instance data, and local data. Storage is assigned for a data value for its lifetime. Class data fields are those that are modified by the keyword static. They belong to the class as a whole, not to an instance of a class, and exist as long as the application is running. Instance fields are those that belong to an instance of the class. These are the class fields that are not modified by static. There is one copy of each field for each instance of the class; that is, each call to new creates these fields. Instance data exists as long as the object in which it is defined exists. Local data fields are those declared within a method. They exist only as long as the method in which they are defined is executing.

Packages

Packages are like classes: We have been using them from the beginning, now we look at how to create them. Recall that a package is a named collection of related classes. Classes within a package can access each other's nonprivate members and can be compiled separately and imported into a program.

To create a package, we just use the keyword package and a package name. By convention, package names begin with a lowercase letter. For example

```
package finances;
```

creates a package named finances. After this statement, we can have an import statement (if needed) and a series of class definitions, making up a *compilation unit*. Only one of the classes in a compilation unit can be declared public and none can be declared private or protected. Any program that wants to use classes in this package uses an *import* statement.

```
import finances;
```

Another important principle in designing classes is *abstraction*, the separation of the logical properties of an object from its implementation. By placing classes into packages, the implementation of the class is hidden from the user. The client only knows what is in the interface, a logical description of the public methods.

Program Design

Object-oriented design is a methodology developed for large-scale programming projects. The solution to a problem using this technique is expressed in terms of self-contained entities called *objects*, which are composed of both data and operations that manipulate the data. Object-oriented design focuses on the objects and their interactions within a problem. Inheritance is a property of object-oriented design in which objects can inherit data and behavior from other objects.

There are four stages to object-oriented problem solving. *Brainstorming* is the stage in which you make a first pass at determining the classes of objects in the problem. *Filtering* is the stage in which you go back over the proposed classes determined in the brainstorming stage to see if any can be combined or if any

Class Name:	Superclass:	Subclasses:
Responsibilities	**Collaborations**	

are missing. *Scenarios* is the stage in which the responsibilities for the classes are determined. In this stage, "what if" questions are explored to be sure that all situations are examined. During this stage, CRC cards (*C*lass, *R*esponsibility, *C*ollaboration) are written for each class of object. *Responsibility Algorithms*, the last stage, is where the algorithms are written for each of the responsibilities outlined on the CRC cards. A CRC card is just a 5 by 8 card with appropriate headings where information about a class can be written. We cover superclasses and subclasses in Laboratory 7.

Functional design (also called top-down or structured design) is like writing an outline for a paper. The main subheadings are listed, and then each subhead is further divided until no more subheadings are needed. In a functional design, the main subheadings are the tasks that must be accomplished for the problem to be solved. Each task (subheading) is further divided into the subtasks that must be accomplished before it is complete. Each subtask is further divided into the tasks necessary to complete its job. A task (or subtask) needs no further division when it becomes a concrete step, that is, when the task (or subtask) can be directly coded into a statement in a programming language.

Function design is often used to write the responsibility algorithms determined during an object-oriented design.

To summarize, functional design methods focus on the *process* of transforming the input into the output, resulting in a hierarchy of tasks. Object-oriented design focuses on the *data objects* that are to be transformed, resulting in a hierarchy of objects. Grady Booch puts it this way: "Read the specification of the software you want to build. Underline the verbs if you are after procedural code, the nouns if you aim for an object-oriented program."[1]

We propose that you circle the nouns and underline the verbs. The nouns become objects; the verbs become operations. In a functional design, the verbs are the primary focus; in an object-oriented design, the nouns are the primary focus.

---

[1] Grady Booch, "What Is and Isn't Objected-Oriented Design." *American Programmer*, special issue on object orientation, vol. 2, no. 7–8, Summer 1989.

Laboratory 6: Prelab Assignment

Name _____ Date _____

Section _____

Use program Money for Exercises 1, 2, and 3.

```java
package money;
public class Money
{
  // Data fields
  public static final char SYMBOL = "$";
  private long dollars;
  private long cents;
  public  Money()

  // Constructor:  Sets dollars and cents to 0
  {
    dollars = 0;
    cents   = 0;
  }

  public Money(long initDollars, long initCents)
  // Constructor: Sets dollars and cents to parameter values
  {
    dollars = initDollars;
    cents   = initCents;
  }

  public void  initialize(long newDollars, long newCents)
  // Initializes dollars and cents
  {
    dollars = newDollars;
    cents = newCents;
  }

  public long  dollarsAre()
  // Returns dollars
  {
    return dollars;
  }

  public long  centsAre()
  // Returns cents
  {
    return cents;
  }
```

```
    public void print()
    // Prints dollars and cents on System.out
    {
      System.out.print("" + Money.SYMBOL + dollars + '.'
        + cents);
    }

    public Money  add(Money  value)
    // Returns sum of object plus value.
    {
      Money  result = new Money();
      result.cents = cents + value.cents;
      result.dollars = dollars + value.dollars;
      return result;
    }
}

import money.*;

public class UseMoney
{
  public static void main(String[] args)
  {
    Money  money1;
    Money  money2;
    Money  money3;
    money1 = new Money(10, 59);
    money2 = new Money(20, 70);
    money3 = money1.add(money2);
    System.out.println("" + SYMBOL + money3.dollarsAre() + '.'
      + money3.centsAre());
  }
}
```

Exercise 1: What is printed by class `UseMoney`?

Exercise 2: Why does method `add` have only one parameter?

Exercise 3: The definition of class `Money` is encapsulated in package `money`. Class `UseMoney` imports this package and manipulates objects of class `Money`. List the class data, instance data, and local data in application `UseMoney`.

Class data fields:

Instance data fields:

Local data fields:

Lesson 6-1: Check Prelab Exercises

Name _____ Date _____

Section _____

Exercise 1: Run program `UseMoney` to check your answer to Exercise 1. Was your answer correct? If not, do you understand where you made your mistake?

Exercise 2: The second parameter for the `add` operation is the object to which the method is being applied.

Exercise 3:

Class data field: `SYMBOL`

Instance data fields: `dollars` and `cents`

Local data fields: There are no local data fields.

Lesson 6-2: Classes

Name _____   Date _____

Section _____

Use class `MessageGenerator` for Exercises 1 – 4.

```
package message;
public class MessageGenerator
{
  /* TO BE FILLED IN: Exercise 1 */

  /* TO BE FILLED IN: Exercise 2 */

  /* TO BE FILLED IN: Exercise 3 */

  /* TO BE FILLED IN: Exercise 4 */
}
```

Exercise 1: Define two class constants: HALF_STOP, which contains a semicolon, and FULL_STOP, which contains a period.

Exercise 2: Define a `String` instance variable `border`.

Exercise 3: Define a method `initialize` with a `String` parameter `newBorder` that stores `newBorder` in `border`.

Exercise 4: Define a method named `printBorder` that prints `border` on `System.out`.

Lesson 6-3: Constructors

Name _____   Date _____

Section _____

Continue to use class `MessageGenerator` for Exercises 1-4.

Exercise 1: Add a default constructor to class `MessageGenerator` to store four blanks in `border`.

Exercise 2: Add a constructor that takes a `String` parameter and stores the parameter in `border`.

Exercise 3: Add a constructor that takes a `String` parameter and an `int` parameter. The string is stored in `border` and printed on `System.out` either 1 or 2 times depending on the value of the parameter. If the integer parameter is not a 1 or a 2, print an error message on `System.out`.

Exercise 4: This lesson defines three constructors. How does the system determine which one to use?

Lesson 6-4: Methods and Parameters

Name _____   Date _____

Section _____

Continue to use class `MessageGenerator` for Exercises 1–4.

Exercise 1: Define a method `writePhrase` that has one `String` parameter. The method should write the parameter on `System.out` followed by HALF_STOP.

Exercise 2: Define a method `writeSentence` that has one `String` parameter. The method should write the parameter on `System.out` followed by FULL_STOP.

Exercise 3: Write an application that imports `MessageGenerator` and uses it to write the following message with a border of plus signs above and below.

> There was a little girl who had a little curl right in the middle of her forehead.
> When she was good, she was very very good;
> When she was bad, she was horrid.

Exercise 4: Add a method, normalize, to class Money that normalizes the cents to between 0 and 99 and adjusts the dollar amount accordingly. Alter program UseMoney from the Prelab lesson to apply method normalize to money3 before printing it. Run the revised program UseMoney. What is printed?

Lesson 6-5: Program Design

Name _____ Date _11/22/04_

Section _____

Exercise 1: You love to travel, and you love to take photographs. When you finish this course, you are going to write a program to keep track of your photograph collection. You plan to use an object-oriented design for your program. In preparation for this project, list a tentative set of objects (the brainstorming stage). Give a list of possible classes. (You are at the talking stage, don't even think about implementation details.)

Folder stores all your pictures → Album   date/time → month, day, year, time
                                                                          ↓
← destinations   hour min → A.M. PM.

country city   Memories → topic/description
                      Companions → who I was with when took picture
                      photographs

Exercise 2: Take this list of tentative topics and filter them, combining or adding new ones. What is your list now?

Exercise 3: Go through some scenarios with your classes assigning responsibilities. Make up CRC cards for your classes. Add more if you need them.

Class Name: destination	Superclass: Album	Subclasses: Pictures
Responsibilities	**Collaborations**	
know memories		
know Companions		
know country		
know city		

Class Name: *Photograph*	Superclass: *Album*	Subclasses:
Responsibilities *Know date*		Collaborations
Know time		*get info for for date*
Know photo descrip.		*get info for time*

Class Name:	Superclass:	Subclasses:
Responsibilities		Collaborations

Exercise 4: Write a functional design for the following problem. Maggie, your Labrador puppy, has eaten a hole in the carpet in the dining room. How much does it cost to replace the carpet? The input to your program should be the dimensions of the room and the price of carpet. The output should be the cost written to the screen. Be sure to include prompts and echo-print the input along with the answer appropriately labeled.

Functional Design

Main   *Level 0*

On a separate sheet of paper, fill in as many levels of detail as are needed to make each statement a concrete step.

Exercise 5: Translate your functional design into Java code and run your program.

Show your input.

How much does it cost to recarpet the dining room?

Lesson 6-6: Debugging

Name _____ Date _____

Section _____

Exercise 1: Program UseMystery is a version of one of the programs that you have been working with in this lesson. Unfortunately, it is buggy. Debug and run the program. Describe the bugs you found.

Exercise 2: Mystery is an alias for which class?

Postlab Activities

Exercise 1: The dining room looks so nice with the new carpet that you decide to repaint the room. Write a design for a program that takes as input the dimensions of the room, the price of a gallon of paint, and the number of square feet that a gallon of paint covers. The output is what it will cost to paint the dining room.

Exercise 2: Translate your design into a Java program and run it.

Exercise 3: Write a design and a Java program to calculate how many calories your lunch contained. Prompt the user to enter the number of calories for meats, the number of calories for starches, and the number of calories for sweets. Have the user press a button when all of the data values have been keyed in. Write the number of total calories on System.out.

Exercise 4: Here is a listing of the public interface of an abstract data type that represents fractions:

```java
public class Fraction
{
  // Methods
  public Fraction  add(Fraction  frac1)
  // Returns object plus frac1

  public Fraction  sub(Fraction  frac1)
  // Returns object minus frac1

  public Fraction  mult(Fraction  frac1)
  // Returns object times frac1

  public Fraction  div(Fraction  frac1)
  // Returns object divided by frac1

  public int  numIs()
  // Returns numerator of frac1

  public int  denomIs()
  // Returns denominator of frac1

  public Fraction(int  num, int  denom);
  // Constructor: sets numerator and denominator

  // Data members
  private int  numerator;
  private int  denominator;
}
```

Implement the methods in class Fraction.

Exercise 5: Write a test plan for class Fraction.

Exercise 6: Write a command-driven driver to implement the test plan written for Exercise 5. A command-driven program is one in which the user enters the operation to be tested followed by the values to use in the test. For example, to test if the add method correctly adds 1/2 and 3/4, the user might input

+ 1 2 3 4

The operation is invoked with the appropriate data, and the result is written on the screen. The user is prompted to enter another operation or quit.

Inheritance, Polymorphism, and Scope

■ To be able to define a class in which a private member is of an existing class.

■ To be able to derive a class from an existing class.

■ To be able to declare and use derived-class objects.

■ To be able to define a class hierarchy in which methods are overridden.

■ To be able to implement a shallow copy constructor and a deep copy constructor.

■ To be able to create, write, and read files of objects.

Laboratory 7: Assignment Cover Sheet

Name _____ Date _____

Section _____

Fill in the following table showing which exercises have been assigned for each lesson and check what you are to submit: (1) lab sheets, (2) listings of output files, and/or (3) listings of code. Your instructor or teaching assistant (TA) can use the Completed column for grading purposes.

Activities	Assigned: Check or list exercise numbers	Submit (1)	(2)	(3)	Completed
Prelab					
Review					
Prelab Assignment					
Inlab					
Lesson 7-1: Check Prelab Exercises					
Lesson 7-2: Classes					
Lesson 7-3: Classes with Inheritance					
Lesson 7-4: Overloading					
Lesson 7-5: Copy Constructors					
Lesson 7-6: Object Output and Input					
Lesson 7-7: Debugging					
Postlab					

Prelab Activities

Review

Objects may be related to one another in one of two ways. An object may be a descendant of another object and inherit the ancestor's properties, or it may include another object as a member. The first is called *inheritance*, and the second is called *composition* or *containment*.

Inheritance

In Java, classes can inherit data and actions from another class. For example, to extend class `Money` defined in Laboratory 6 to include a field that says whether the money is real money or play money, we define a class that inherits from `Money`. A summary of class `Money` is shown below. A summary is a listing of the methods that a user can access. Note that this is a form of documentation, not a syntactic structure.

```java
public class Money
{
  public Money();                    // Default constructor
  public Money(long initDollars, long initCents)
  public void initialize(long newDollars, long newCents)
  public long dollarsAre()
  public long centsAre()
  public Money add(Money  value)
  public void print()
}
```

Here is the listing of class `ExtMoney`, a class derived from class `Money`.

```java
class ExtMoney extends Money
{
  private String kindOfMoney;

  public ExtMoney()
  // Constructor: default kind is "real"
  {
    super();
    kindOfMoney = "real";
  }
  public ExtMoney
     (long newDollars, long newCents, String newKind)
  // Constructor: kind set to newCurrency
  {
    super(newDollars, newCents);
    kindOfMoney = newKind;
  }
  public void initialize
     (long newDollars, long newCents, String newKind)
  {
    super(newDollars, newCents);
```

```
      kindOfMoney = newKind;
  }

  public String kindIs()
  {
    return kindOfMoney;
  }

  public void print()
  {
    super.print();
    System.out.println(" is " + kindOfMoney);
  }
}
```

The phrase `extends Money` says that the new class being defined (`ExtMoney`) is inheriting the members of class `Money`. `ExtMoney` has three member variables: one of its own (`kindOfMoney`) and two that it inherits from `Money` (`dollars` and `cents`). `ExtMoney` has seven methods: three of its own (`initialize`, `kindIs`, and `print`) and four that it inherits from `Money` (`initialize`, `dollarsAre`, `centsAre`, and `add`). In addition, `ExtMoney` has two constructors. Constructors cannot be inherited, but the superclass constructor can be invoked by the expression `super()` with the appropriate parameters.

Hiding and Overriding

`Money` is called the *base* class or *super* class; it is the class being derived from. `ExtMoney` is the *derived* class or *subclass*; it is the one being derived. Both `Money` and `ExtMoney` have a method `initialize`. Using the same name is called *overloading*. Because their parameter lists are different, the compiler has no trouble determining which one is being invoked. We say that they have different *signatures*. A method's signature is the name and a list of the parameter types in the order that they appear on the parameter list. Both classes have a method `print` with the same signature. If an instance method in a derived class has the same signature as an instance method in the base class, the derived class method *overrides* the base class method. This means that the derived class method redefines the method in the superclass. `ExtMoney` redefines the print method: The overridden method is called and then the kind is written.

As we saw in this example, fields are inherited as well as methods. If a derived class defines a field with the same name as one in the superclass, the derived field *hides* the one in the superclass. A derived class may have a method with the same signature as a class method in the superclass, but Java considers that a form of hiding rather than overriding, although the derived method does redefine the superclass method.

The ability of a language to have duplicate method names in a hierarchy of derived classes and to choose the appropriate method based on the type of the object to which the method is applied is called *polymorphism*.

`super` is a keyword that allows a derived class to access nonprivate hidden or overridden methods and fields. `super` and a dot preceding a hidden or overridden identifier refers to the identifier in the superclass. `super` is also used to access a superclass constructor as shown in the constructors for `ExtMoney`.

Scope

Scope, short for scope of access, determines where identifiers are accessible. There are two kinds of scope: internal and external. Internal refers to scope within a class; external refers to scope outside of a class.

Scope rules within a class do not depend on the access modifiers and are very simple. Any class identifier can be accessed from anywhere within the class. There are two exceptions to this rule. The first is that an uninitialized class variable cannot be used to initialize another variable. The second involves shadowing, the scope rule that says that if there is a local identifier and a class identifier with the same name, the local identifier takes precedence. The scope of a local identifier is from the point of its declaration to the end of the block in which it is declared.

If for some reason you need to reference a member hidden by a local member, the keyword `this` preceding the member with a dot in between allows you to access it. Look at the following example.

```
public class ScopeExample
{
   private static int oneVariable;
   private static int anotherVariable;
   public static void aMethod()
   {
      int oneVariable;
      anotherVariable = 20;
      oneVariable = 25;
      this.oneVariable = 60;
   }
   ...
}
```

`oneVariable` exists as a class variable and as a local variable. Within `aMethod`, `oneVariable` refers to the local variable, and `anotherVariable` refers to the class variable because there is no local variable with the same name. Within `aMethod`, `this.oneVariable` refers to the class variable rather than the local variable of the same name.

The external scope rules determine access to class members from without the class. There are three places where members of a class can be accessed: from a derived class, from classes in the same package, and from a class not in the same package. The modifiers `private`, `public`, and `protected` are called access modifiers. If no access modifier is specified for a member, it is package access. The scope rules are reflected in the meaning of these modifiers.

Private access is the most restricted. Only members in the same class can access members marked `private`. *Package* access refers to members, defined within classes in the same package, that do not have an access modifier. Such members may be accessed from all classes in the same package. *Protected* access refers to members marked `protected`. These members are accessible to classes in the same package and can be inherited by derived classes outside the package. *Public* access is the least restrictive: Any member marked `public` can be accessed from any class.

Class members marked `public` or `protected` can be inherited in a derived class. A derived class that is outside the package in which a `protected` member is defined can inherit the `protected` member, but it cannot access it directly.

Abstract Modifier

There is another important modifier that relates to inheritance: `abstract`. If a class is marked `abstract`, it means that it is incomplete, that there is one or more class methods that have not been defined. An undefined method is one that is marked `abstract` and just has the signature followed by a semicolon instead of a method body. If there is an undefined method, the class must be marked `abstract`. An abstract class cannot be instantiated. Any class that is derived from an abstract class must fill in the body of all the undefined methods or the derived class is also abstract.

Copy Constructors

A copy constructor is a constructor that takes an instance of the object as a parameter and returns a copy. Syntactically a copy constructor looks just like any other constructor except that it has a parameter of its own class. The code within the copy constructor creates and returns a copy of the parameter. The copy constructor may return an identical object or the constructor may make changes depending on what is needed.

If the object being copied contains fields that are themselves reference types, "copy" can have two meanings. Copy can mean to copy the fields exactly without regard to whether they are primitive or reference types (a shallow copy) or it can mean to copy primitive fields and then make a copy of what the reference fields reference (a deep copy).

Object Output and Input

All the input and output we have used so far have been based on a stream of characters. Java has a couple of classes based on a stream of objects: `ObjectOutputStream` derived from `OutputStream` and `ObjectInputStream` derived from `InputStream`. Method `writeObject` applied to a file writes the object as a unit of data. Method `readObject` applied to a file reads an object as the unit of data. To read an object, it must have been written as an object. Therefore, writing must come before reading.

Serializing is the translation from an object to a sequence of bytes. Deserializing is the translation from a sequence of bytes to an object. For an object to be written using the `writeObject` method, its class must implement the `Serializable` interface. Here is a program that writes out objects of class `Money` and then one that reads them back in.

```
// Class MoneyWrite writes out Money objects
import java.io.*;
import money.*;
// import money.*; Implements Serializable

public class MoneyWrite
{
  private static ObjectOutputStream outObject;
  // Output data file

  public static void main(String[] args)
    throws IOException
  {
    outObject = new ObjectOutputStream
      (new FileOutputStream("outMoney.dat"));
```

```
    // Create and write two Money objects
    Money someMoney = new Money(222, 33);
    outObject.writeObject(someMoney);
    Money moreMoney = new Money(333, 22);
    outObject.writeObject(moreMoney);
    outObject.close();
  }
}

// Class MoneyRead reads in Money objects
import java.io.*;
import money;
public class MoneyRead
{
  private static ObjectInputStream inObject;
  // Input file

  public static void main(String[] args)
   throws IOException, ClassNotFoundException
  {
    Money someMoney;

    // Prepare file
    inObject = new ObjectInputStream
      (new FileInputStream("outMoney.dat"));

    // Read and print two Money objects
    someMoney = (Money)inObject.readObject();
    System.out.println("Dollars: " +
     someMoney.dollarsAre() +
      " Cents: " + someMoney.centsAre());
    someMoney = (Money)inObject.readObject();
    System.out.println("Dollars: " +
      someMoney.dollarsAre() +
      " Cents: " + someMoney.centsAre());

    inObject.close();
  }
}
```

When the object is being read in, the code needs to know which class it is. Therefore the object that is returned by readObject must be type cast back into the right class, Money in this case.

Laboratory 7: Prelab Assignment

Name _____   Date _____

Section _____

Read the following class summaries carefully.

```
public class Money
{
  public Money()                  // Default constructor
  public Money(long initDollars, long initCents)
  public void initialize(long newDollars, long newCents)
  public long dollarsAre()
  public long centsAre()
  public Money add(Money  value)
  public void print()
}

public class ExtMoney extends Money
{
  public ExtMoney()
  public ExtMoney
    (long newDollars, long newCents, String kind)
  public void initialize
    (long newDollars, long newCents, String kind)
  public String kindIs()
  public void print()
}
```

```
import money.Money;
import extMoney.ExtMoney;
public class UseMoney
// A driver class using Money and ExtMoney
{
  public static void main(String[] args)
  {
    Money money1;
    Money money2;
    ExtMoney extMoney1;
    ExtMoney extMoney2;

    System.out.println("Initialized by default constructors");
    money1 = new Money();
    extMoney1 = new ExtMoney();
    System.out.println("variables instantiated");
    money1.print();
    extMoney1.print();

    System.out.println("Initialized by other constructor");
    money2 = new Money(2000, 22);
    extMoney2 = new ExtMoney(3000, 88, "monopoly");
```

```
        money2.print();

        extMoney2.print();

        System.out.println("initialized at run time");
        money1.initialize(4000, 44);
        extMoney1.initialize(5000, 99, "play");
        money1.print();
        extMoney1.print();
    }
}
```

Exercise 1: What is printed?

Exercise 2: List the overloaded identifiers.

Exercise 3: List the overridden identifiers.

Exercise 4: List the hidden identifiers.

Exercise 5: Why did we just show the class summary?

Lesson 7–1: Check Prelab Exercises

Name _____ Date _____

Section _____

Exercise 1: Run program `UseMoney` to check your answers. Were they correct? Explain.

Exercise 2: `initialize` and `print`

Exercise 3: `print`

Exercise 4: There are no hidden identifiers.

Exercise 5: You do not need to see the complete classes to understand what a program is doing. The information for the user (the client program) is in the summaries.

Lesson 7-2: Classes

Name _____ Date _____

Section _____

Exercise 1: Complete the method bodies for class `Date`.

```
package date;
public class Date
{
  // Data fields
  private int day;
  private int year;
  private String month;

  // Methods
  public Date(int newDay, String newMonth, int newYear)
  {
    /* TO BE FILLED IN */
  }
  public int dayIs()
  {
    /* TO BE FILLED IN */
  }
  public String monthIs()
  {
    /* TO BE FILLED IN */
  }
  public int yearIs()
  {
    /* TO BE FILLED IN */
  }
  public void print()
  // Output on System.out
  {
    /* TO BE FILLED IN */
  }
}
```

Exercise 2: Write a driver to test class `Date`, using December 6, 1944. Show your output.

Exercise 3: Write the Java class for the following CRC card class description.

Class Name: Car		Superclass:		Subclasses:
Responsibilities		**Collaborations**		
Create itself(dealer cost, id Number, date arrived)		Date		
Know dealer cost return float		None		
Know id number return int		None		
Know date arrived return Date		Date		
Print		Date, System.out		

Exercise 4: Write a driver to test class `Car`. Use the following values.

        dealer cost   14,000
        id number   1245632
        date arrived October 11, 2001
Show your output.

Lesson 7-3: Classes with Inheritance

Name _____ Date _____

Section _____

Exercise 1: Derive a new class from class Car, using this CRC card class description.

Class Name: Sold car	Superclass: Car	Subclasses:
Responsibilities	**Collaborations**	
Create itself(dealer cost, id number, date arrived, price, customer, date sold)	Date, Car	
Create itself(car, price, customer, date sold)	Date, Car	
Know price return float	None	
Know customer return String	String	
Know date sold return Date	Date	
Calculate profit return float	None	
Print	Date, car, system.out	

Exercise 2: Write a driver to test class SoldCar. Describe your data and show the output.

Lesson 7-4: Overloading

Name _____ Date _____

Section _____

Exercises 1 through 4 use application Driver.

```
import cars.*;        // Access Date, Car, and SoldCar classes

public class Driver
{
  public static void main(String[] args)
  {
    /* TO BE FILLED IN: Exercise 1 */
    /* TO BE FILLED IN: Exercise 2 */
    /* TO BE FILLED IN: Exercise 3 */
    /* TO BE FILLED IN: Exercise 4 */
  }
}
```

Exercise 1: Declare the following objects.

identifier	class
date	Date
car	Car
myCar	SoldCar
yourCar	SoldCar

Exercise 2: Instantiate the variables declared in Exercise 1. Show the values you used with each constructor, using car to instantiate yourCar.

Exercise 3: Apply method print to each of the objects declared in Exercise 1. Show what is printed.

Exercise 4: Write on System.out the profit the dealer made selling yourCar. Show your output.

Lesson 7-5: Copy Constructors

Name _____ Date _____

Section _____

Exercise 1: Add two copy constructors to class `CarSold`, one that performs a shallow copy and one that performs a deep copy.

Exercise 2: Add the following method to class `CarSold`.

```
public void allCaps()
{
   customer = customer.toUpperCase();
}
```

If you called `customer` something else, just substitute your name.

Exercise 3: Write a driver that does the following tasks.

Instantiate `carOne` with the customer name of "Monika Moonlight".

Print `carOne`.

Copy `carOne` into `carTwo`, using a shallow copy.

Copy `carOne` into `carThree`, using a deep copy.

Print `carTwo` and `carThree`.

Apply `allCaps` to `carOne`.

Print `carTwo` and `carThree`.

Describe the results, showing what is printed.

Lesson 7-6: Object Output and Input

Name _____ Date _____

Section _____

Exercise 1: Take the code that you wrote in Lesson 7-4, instantiate a third object, and write the objects to object file `carObjectFile`.

Exercise 2: Write an application that reads the file written in Exercise 1 and prints the values using method `print`. What is printed?

Lesson 7-7: Debugging

Name _____ Date _____

Section _____

Exercise 1: Class UseMystery is a client program that uses class Money and a class Mystery. Find the errors and correct them. Describe the errors.

Postlab Activities

Exercise 1: Design a class that represents a dog. This class should have fields that represent the breed, the weight, the sex, and the birth date. Represent your design in a CRC card.

Class Name:	Superclass:	Subclasses:
Responsibilities		Collaborations

Exercise 2: Implement the class designed in Exercise 1.

Exercise 3: Write a test driver to test class Dog. Make your driver interactive. Have the user enter the information in a window.

Exercise 4: Derive class PetDog from class Dog. This class should have fields for owner and address. Write a test plan and driver to test your class.

Exercise 5: Derive a second class from class Dog named WorkingDog. This class should have fields for business name, address, and kind of work. Write a test plan and driver to test your class.

Event–Driven Input and Output

- To be able to construct a code segment that creates a `JFrame` window on the screen.

- To be able to construct a code segment that displays a message in a window on the screen.

- To be able to use a layout manager to organize messages in a window.

- To be able to use a `JTextField` to input a value.

- To be able to write an event handler for a single button.

- To be able to write an event handler that distinguishes among multiple event sources.

Laboratory 8: Assignment Cover Sheet

Name _____ Date _____

Section _____

Fill in the following table showing which exercises have been assigned for each lesson and check what you are to submit: (1) lab sheets, (2) listings of output files, and/or (3) listings of code. Your instructor or teaching assistant (TA) can use the Completed column for grading purposes.

Activities	Assigned: Check or list exercise numbers	Submit (1) (2) (3)			Completed
Prelab					
Review					
Prelab Assignment					
Inlab					
Lesson 8-1: Check Prelab Exercises					
Lesson 8-2: Window Ouput					
Lesson 8-3: Labels and Data Entry Fields					
Lesson 8-4: Button Events					
Lesson 8-5: Multiple Button Events					
Postlab					

Prelab Activities

Review

Up until now, we have been using `System.in` for input and `System.out` for output. In this chapter, we examine how to create windows on the screen, put objects into the windows, and extract values from the windows. The type of window that we use is called a *frame*.

Frames

A class is a pattern for an object. The class that is the pattern for the window object is the `JFrame` class. In order to declare and manipulate an object of this type, we must import this class and several others that are available in packages `java.awt`, `java.awt.event`, and `javax.swing`. We declare a variable of class `JFrame` just like we declare a variable of any other type.

```
JFrame ourFrame;
```

and instantiate it just like any other class object

```
ourFrame = new JFrame();
```

Now that we have a frame, we must set its size and specify what action to take when the frame is closed.

```
ourFrame.setSize(300, 200);
ourFrame.setDefaultCloseOperation(JFrame.EXIT_ON_CLOSE);
```

The next step is to get a container (called a pane) from the frame into which we can put other objects such as labels and buttons.

```
ourPane = ourFrame.getContentPane();
```

Once we have a content pane, we can begin putting other objects into it, but before we do, we need to tell the pane how we want it to look. There is a method we can use for this purpose: `setLayout`. If the parameter to `setLayout` is an object of class `FlowLayout`, the pane places as many components on a row as possible before going to the next row. If the parameter is an object of class `GridLayout`, the pane has as many rows and columns as are listed in `GridLayout`'s parameters. The first statement lets the pane decide; the second says to have 3 rows and 4 columns.

```
ourPane.setLayout(new FlowLayout());
ourPane.setLayout(new GridLayout(3, 4);
```

For obvious reasons, `FlowLayout` and `GridLayout` are called layout manager classes. Notice that we had to instantiate each before we could pass it as a parameter.

Text objects that are put into the pane are objects of class `JLabel`. We can declare and instantiate them and then put them in the pane, or we can instantiate them anonymously as we are putting them in the pane. We use the `add` method to put objects into the pane.

```
JLabel ourLabel;
ourLabel = new JLabel("Happy New Year");
ourPane.add(ourLabel);
ourPane.add(new JLabel("Cheers!"));
```

We have only one task left: to make the window visible.

```
ourFrame.setVisible(true);
```

Frame Input

The object in a content pane into which data can be keyed by the user and accessed by the application is an object of class `JTextField`.

```
private static JTextField message;
message = new JTextField(20);
```

`JTextField` is the name of the class that describes a place where the user can enter data. The constructor for the class shown in this example takes an integer parameter that specifies how many character positions should be in the data field. An alternative constructor allows you to place a string in the data field as well as specify the number of characters.

```
message = new JTextField("Replace me", 10);
```

Now that we have a data entry field, we should label it so that the user can tell what it is for and add it to the pane.

```
ourPane.add(new JLabel("Enter the message"));
ourPane.add(message);
```

These statements add the label and the data entry field. The user clicks the data entry field (the instance of `JTextField`) and then starts typing.

Class `JTextField` has two very useful methods defined within it: `getText` and `setText`. `getText` is a value-returning method that returns the string of characters that the user typed into the field; `setText` is a void method that allows the program to write a value into the data entry field. (The `JLabel` class also has a `setText` method so that the program can change the characters in a label as well.)

Buttons and Events

We have shown how to create a data entry field and get the string from the field. We have skipped one important question: *How does the program know when the user has finished inputting the data?* We need to create a button that the user can click to tell the application that the data is ready to be read.

Adding a button to a pane is just like adding a label or a data entry field to a pane: We declare a button variable, we instantiate the button object, and we add it to the pane.

```
JButton ourButton;
ourButton = new JButton("Enter");
ourPane.add(ourButton);
```

The string "Enter" appears under the button on the screen and also names the button within the system. Now we must tell the system what to do when the button is pushed.

When a button is pushed, we say that an event has occurred. *Event listeners* are objects whose role in life is to wait for an event to occur. We have to hook up an object that can cause (fire) an event with an object that is listening for the event to occur. The object that is listening for the event is an object of a class that implements the `ActionListener` interface and has a special method called `actionPerformed`.

```
private static class OurListener implements ActionListener
{
  public void actionPerformed(ActionEvent ourEvent)
  {
    String ourMessage;
    ourMessage = message.getText();
    // Display message
    System.out.println(ourMessage);
    message.setText("Thanks");
  }
}
```

The only thing we can change in this pattern is the name of the class. The body of the `actionPerformed` method is where we put the code to be executed when the user pushes the button. Did you notice that we declared `message` to be `static` and `private`? `message` is accessed in method `actionPerformed`. Therefore `message` must be declared where `actionPerformed` can access it. If the listener class is declared within the application, `message` must be declared within the same block, not hidden within the `main` method.

We now have a button object and a button listener class. We tie these pieces together by declaring a variable of the listener class, instantiating the listener, and registering the listener with the button (the event source).

```
ourListener listener;                       // Declare listener
listener = new ourListener();               // Instantiate listener
// Connect button and listener
ourButton.addActionListener(listener);
```

When the application is all put together, remember that any object referenced in the listener must be declared where it is visible to the listener.

Look back at class `OurListener`. What do you think happens when "Thanks" has been written in the pane? The listener quietly waits for the user to enter another text message. Theoretically, the application could run forever. The user can stop the process by closing the window or stopping the application, or we could end the method with `System.exit(0)`. Such a loop is called an *event loop*.

An alternative to this approach is to give the user more than one button. For example, we can put two buttons on the screen: "Enter" and "Stop". The user is prompted to continue entering data and pressing the "Enter" button until all data has been entered, at which time the user should press "Stop". The two buttons are declared and instantiated, and the listener is registered with both, using the addActionListener method. When either button is pressed, the actionPerformed method in class OurListener is executed.

How does the code know which button was pushed? It asks the listener to tell it. The actionPerformed method has a parameter of class ActionEvent that we called ourEvent. When the event source invokes the actionPerformed method in the listener, it sends its name to the method through the argument. The actionPerformed method can access the button's name using the getActionCommand method applied to the parameter. The following code segment

```
String name;
name = ourEvent.getActionCommand();
```

stores the name of the button in name.

Laboratory 8: Prelab Assignment

Name _____   Date _____

Section _____

Examine the following program carefully and answer the questions.

```java
//*********************************************************************
// Display Message application demonstrates how to create a JFrame,
//  get a pane, put labels in the pane, and display the pane.
//*********************************************************************
import java.awt.*;         // Accesses layout manager
import javax.swing.*;      // Accesses JFrame class for our display
public class DisplayMessage
{
  public static void main(String[] args)
  {
    final String HOLIDAY  = "New Year's Eve";      // A holiday
    final String MESSAGE  = "Happy New Year";      // A message
    JLabel ourLabel;

    JFrame ourFrame;                        // Declare JFrame object
    Container ourPane;                      // Declare Container object

    // Create a JFrame object
    ourFrame = new JFrame();
    // Specify the size of the JFrame object
    ourFrame.setSize(300, 200);
    // Specify the action to take when the window is closed
    ourFrame.setDefaultCloseOperation(JFrame.EXIT_ON_CLOSE);

    // Ask the JFrame object to return a Content Pane Container object
    ourPane = ourFrame.getContentPane();
    // Specify a layout manager for the Content Pane object
    ourPane.setLayout(new FlowLayout());

    // Add output to the content pane
    ourLabel = new JLabel("Holiday is " + HOLIDAY);
    // Instantiate a label
    ourPane.add(ourLabel);

    // Display message
    ourPane.add(new JLabel("Message is " + MESSAGE));

    // Make the JFrame object visible on the screen
    ourFrame.setVisible(true);
  }
}
```

Exercise 1: List the class and variable of all the objects in the pane.

Exercise 2: Describe the window, showing what is printed.

Examine the following program carefully and answer the questions.

```
//*************************************************************
// PrintInput application demonstrates how to create a JFrame,
//   put labels and text boxes in the frame, and input values
//   from the text box.
//*************************************************************
import java.awt.*;       // Accesses layout manager
import javax.swing.*;   // Accesses JFrame class for our display
import java.awt.event.*; //Supplies event classes

public class PrintInput
{
  private static class OurListener implements ActionListener
  {
    public void actionPerformed(ActionEvent ourEvent)
    //Event handler method
    {
      String ourMessage;
      ourMessage = message.getText();
      // Display message
      System.out.println(ourMessage);
      message.setText("Thanks");
    }
  }                              //End of OurListener class

  private static JTextField message;     // Input field for message

  public static void main(String[] args)
  {
    JButton ourButton;
    JFrame ourFrame;                     // Declare JFrame object
    Container ourPane;                   // Declare Container object
    OurListener listener;
    listener = new OurListener();

    // Create a JFrame object
    ourFrame = new JFrame();
    // Specify the size of the JFrame object
    ourFrame.setSize(300, 200);
    // Specify the action to take when the window is closed
```

```
ourFrame.setDefaultCloseOperation(JFrame.EXIT_ON_CLOSE);

// Ask the JFrame object to return a
// Content Pane Container object
ourPane = ourFrame.getContentPane();
// Specify a layout manager for the Content Pane object
ourPane.setLayout(new FlowLayout());

// Add label to the pane
ourPane.add(new JLabel("Enter the message"));

// Instantiate and add text field to pane
message = new JTextField(20);
ourPane.add(message);

// Instantiate button, register listener with button, and
// add to the pane
ourButton = new JButton("Enter");
ourButton.addActionListener(listener);
ourPane.add(ourButton);

// Make the JFrame object visible on the screen
ourFrame.setVisible(true);
    }
}
```

Exercise 3: Draw the objects in the pane.

Exercise 4: If you enter the string "Good day" and press the button, what is changed in the pane?

Exercise 5: What ended the application?

Lesson 8-1: Check Prelab Exercises

Name _____ Date _____

Section _____

Exercise 1:
```
Container ourPane
JLabel    ourLabel
JLabel    anonymous
```

Exercise 2: Run program `DisplayMessage` to check your answers. Were your answers completely correct? If they were not, explain what was wrong.

Exercises 3 and 4: Run program `PrintInput` to check your answers. Were your answers completely correct? If they were not, explain what was wrong.

Exercise 5: Did you press close the window or stop the application?

Lesson 8-2: Window Output

Name _____ Date _____

Section _____

This lesson uses program `Greet`. Compile and rerun the program after each modification.

```
// Program Greet prints a greeting on the screen
import java.awt.*;
import java.awt.event.*;
import javax.swing.*;
public class Greet
{

  public static void main(String[] args)
  {
     final String MESSAGE = "Good morning ";
     JFrame yourFrame;
     yourFrame = _____ JFrame();
     Container greetDisplay;
     greetDisplay = _____.getContentPane();
     _____.setDefaultCloseOperation(JFrame.EXIT_ON_CLOSE);
     greetDisplay._____(new FlowLayout());
     greetDisplay.add(new _____(MESSAGE));
     greetDisplay.add(_____ JLabel("Sarah "));
     greetDisplay._____(new JLabel("Sunshine"));
     yourFrame.setVisible(_____);
  }
}
```

Exercise 1: Program `Greet` writes a greeting in a window on the screen. However, it is missing certain identifiers, reserved words, and operators that are necessary for it to compile. Replace each blank with the appropriate identifier, reserved word, or operator and run the program. Record the output.

Exercise 2: Change the program in Exercise 1 so that it prints your name instead of "Sarah Sunshine". Compile and run your program. Record your output.

Exercise 3: Change the program in Exercise 2 so that it also prints your birthday on the line under your name. Compile and run your program. Record the output.

Use the following program Shell for Exercises 4 and 5.

```
// Program Shell
import java.awt.*;
import java.awt.event.*;
import javax.swing.*;
public class Shell
{
  public static void main(String[] args)
  {

  }
}
```

Exercise 4: Write the statements necessary to declare, instantiate, and display a pane on the screen. Write whatever message you wish in the window. Compile and run your program. What did the program display in the window?

Exercise 5: Replace your message with the following one.

Roses are red.
Violets are blue.
If I can learn Java,
so can you.

You must use three named constants that contain the strings "roses", "Violets", and "Java". Compile and run your program.

Lesson 8-3: Labels and Data Entry Fields

Name _____ Date _____

Section _____

Use program She112 for this lesson.

```java
import java.awt.*;
import java.awt.event.*;
import javax.swing.*;

public class Shell2
{
  // Listener for button event
  private static class OurListener implements ActionListener
  {
    public void actionPerformed(ActionEvent event)
    {
      String inValue;
      /*  TO BE FILLED IN: Exercise 4 */
    }
  }

  // Declare all variables accessed within the listeners
  private static JFrame outDisplay;

  /* TO BE FILLED IN: Exercise 1*/

  public static void main(String[] args)
  {
    // Other declarations
    JButton button;
    OurListener listener = Our Listener;
    outDisplay = new JFrame();

    /* TO BE FILLED IN: Exercise 2 */
    outDisplay.setSize(300, 200);

    /* TO BE FILLED IN: Exercise 3 */

    button = new JButton("Enter");
    ourPane.add(button);
    listener = new OurListener();
    button.addActionListener(listener);
    // Register listener with window event source

    outDisplay.setVisible(true);

  }
}
```

Exercise 1: Fill in the statements that declare a JTextField and a JLabel.

Exercise 2: Fill in the statements that declare and get a content pane ourPane and set the layout manager to FlowLayout.

Exercise 3: Fill in the statements that instantiate the JTextField with room for 6 columns and the JLabel with the string "Data Entry" and add them to the pane.

Exercise 4: Fill in the statements that take the string that is entered and write it on System.out, appropriately labeled. Compile and run your program.

What is written in the window?

What is written on System.out?

Exercise 5: Add an additional data entry field and label to the application in Exercise 4. Compile and run the program. Enter "Hello" in the first data entry field and "Good night" in the second data entry field. Show your output.

Lesson 8-4: Button Events

Name _____ Date _____

Section _____

Use the Shell3 for this lesson.

```java
import java.awt.*;
import java.awt.event.*;
import javax.swing.*;

public class Shell3
{
  // Listener for button event
  private static class /* TO BE FILLED IN: Exercise 2 */
    implements ActionListener
  {
    public void actionPerformed(ActionEvent event)
    {
      String inString;
      double number;
      inString = dataField.getText();
      /* TO BE INSERTED: Exercise 3 */
      System.out.println(number);
    }
  }
  // Declare all variables accessed within the listeners
  private static JTextField dataField;

  public static void main(String[] args)
  {
    JFrame outWindow;
    Container outPane;
    JLabel prompt;
    /* TO BE FILLED IN: Exercise 1 */
    /* TO BE FILLED IN: Exercise 2 */
    outWindow = new JFrame();
    outWindow.setDefaultCloseOperation(JFrame.EXIT_ON_CLOSE);
    outWindow.setSize(300, 200);
    outPane = outWindow.getContentPane();
    outPane.setLayout(new GridLayout(0, 1));
    dataField = new JTextField("Replace me", 10);
    prompt = new JLabel("Enter data here:");
    outPane.add(dataField);
    outPane.add(prompt);

    /* TO BE FILLED IN: Exercise 2 */

    outWindow.setVisible(true);
  }
}
```

Exercise 1: Insert the statements that declare and instantiate a `JButton` object labeled "Done" and add the button to the pane.

Exercise 2: Insert the statements that name the button listener class, declare and instantiate an object of the listener class, and register the listener class with the button event source.

Exercise 3: Insert the statement that converts a string to a value of type `double`. Compile and run the program. Input the string "999.99". What is displayed where?

Lesson 8–5: Multiple Button Events

Name _____ Date _____

Section _____

Exercise 3, Lesson 4-5, asked you to find the largest of three input values. In this lesson, you are asked to solve the same problem with input coming from a pane. Use `Shell4` for this lesson.

```java
// Program HighScore reads and prints three test scores.
//   The largest value of the three is printed with an
//   appropriate message
// Assumption:  The scores are unique
import java.awt.*;
import java.awt.event.*;
import javax.swing.*;

public class HighScore

{
  private static class ButtonListener
    implements ActionListener
  {
    public void actionPerformed(ActionEvent event)
    {
      /* TO BE FILLED IN */

    }
  }


  private static JTextField score2;
  private static JTextField score3;
  private static JTextField score1;
  private static JButton enter;

  public static void main(String[] args)
  {
    JFrame outWindow;
    Container outPane;
    JLabel prompt = new JLabel("Enter three scores and " +
      "press Enter");
    score1 = new JTextField(4);
    score2 = new JTextField(4);
    score3 = new TextField(4);
    enter = new JButton("Enter");

    /* TO BE FILLED IN */
  }
}
```

Exercise 1: Fill in the missing code, compile, and run the application `HighScore`. What data did you use and what was your answer?

Exercise 2: Application `HighScore` continues to wait for more input until the window is closed or the application is terminated. Add a second button that the user should push when the application is finished. Run the altered program with two sets of data before pushing the second button. What data did you use and what was the output?

Postlab Activities

Exercise 1: Laboratory 3, Postlab Exercise 5, and Laboratory 4, PostLab Exercise 4 relate to calculating the body mass index (BMI) for one person. Write a design and a program that creates a BMI calculator. Design an applet that prompts the user to enter his or her weight in pounds and height in inches. The program should calculate the body mass index (BMI) and display this value and its interpretation in the frame. The formula is

$$BMI = weight * 703 / (height * height)$$

and the interpretation is shown in the following table.

BMI	Interpretation
Under 16	Emaciated
16 – 19	Underweight
20 – 24	Normal
26 – 30	Overweight
Over 30	Obese

The calculator should continue to run until the window is closed or the program is halted.

Exercise 2: Add a second button stop to the program in Exercise 1 that allows the user to stop the program by pressing this button.

Exercise 3: In Exercise 3, Laboratory 4, you wrote an application to test an approximation of a Celsius equivalent of a Fahrenheit temperature. Rewrite this application using window input and output. Create an event loop that continues until the user presses the button marked to stop the processing.

Additional Control Structures and Exceptions

- ■ To be able to convert a series of *if* statements to a *switch* statement.

- ■ To be able to construct a *switch* statement to implement a specified task.

- ■ To be able to convert a *while* loop to a *do* loop.

- ■ To be able to construct a *do* loop to implement a specified task.

- ■ To be able to construct a *for* statement to implement a specified task.

- ■ To be able to construct *try-catch* and *throw* statements to handle exceptions.

- ■ To be able to define and use an exception class.

Laboratory 9 : Assignment Cover Sheet

Name _____ Date _____

Section _____

Fill in the following table showing which exercises have been assigned for each lesson and check what you are to submit: (1) lab sheets, (2) listings of output files, and/or (3) listings of code. Your instructor or teaching assistant (TA) can use the Completed column for grading purposes.

Activities	Assigned: Check or list exercise numbers	Submit (1) (2) (3)			Completed
Prelab					
Review					
Prelab Assignment					
Inlab					
Lesson 9-1: Check Prelab Exercises					
Lesson 9-2: Multi-Way Branching					
Lesson 9-3: Additional Control Structures					
Lesson 9-4: Exception Handling					
Lesson 9-5: Debugging					
Postlab					

Prelab Activities

Review

In preceding chapters, we covered five control structures: the sequence, events, the *if* statement, the *while* statement, and void and value-returning functions. In this chapter, we introduce five additional control structures that make certain tasks easier. However, they represent the icing on the cake. You cannot do anything with them that you cannot do with the control structures that you already know.

Break and Continue

Both *break* and *continue* statements are statements that alter the flow of execution within a control structure. `break` is used with the *switch* statement, the *while* statement, the *do* statement, and the *for* statement. (The *switch*, *do*, and *for* statements are defined below.) `break` interrupts the flow of control by immediately exiting these statements. In contrast, `continue` is used only with looping statements. It alters the flow of control by immediately terminating the current iteration. Note the difference between `continue` and `break` in a loop: `continue` skips to the next iteration of the loop, and `break` skips to the statement following the loop.

    `break` is extremely useful with the *switch* statement but should be used with extreme caution with looping statements. Good style dictates that loops have only one entry and one exit except under very unusual circumstances. `continue` is very seldom used; we only mention it for completeness.

Multi-Way Branching: `switch`

The *switch* statement is a selection statement that can be used in place of a series of *if-else* statements. Alternative statements are listed with a *switch label* in front of each. A *switch* label is either a *case label* or the word `default`. A case label is the word `case` followed by a constant expression. An integral expression called the *switch expression* is used to match one of the values on the case labels. The statement associated with the value that is matched is the statement that is executed. Execution then continues sequentially from the matched label until the end of the *switch* statement is encountered or a `break` statement is encountered.

```
switch (grade)
{
  case 'A' : System.out.println("Great work!");
             break;
  case 'B' : System.out.println("Good work!");
             break;
  case 'C' : System.out.println("Passing work!");
             break;
  case 'D' :
  case 'F' : System.out.println("Unsatisfactory work."
               + "See your instructor.");
             break;
  default  : System.out.println(grade +
```

```
            " is not a legal grade";
        break;
}
```

grade is the *switch* expression; the letters beside the statements make up the case labels. The value in grade is compared with the value in each case label. When a match is found, the corresponding statement is executed. If the value of the *switch* expression does not match a value in any case label, the default label is matched by default. Because execution continues after a match until break is encountered, both 'D' and 'F' send the same message to the screen. What would happen if we forgot to put break after the statement associated with case 'B'? Every time grade contained a "B" both "Good work!" and "Passing work!" would be printed.

Looping: do

The *do* statement is a looping statement that tests the Boolean expression at the end of the loop. A statement (or sequence of statements) is executed while an expression is true. The *do* statement differs from the *while* statement in one major respect: The body of the loop is always executed at least once in the *do* statement. For example, the following loop reads and counts lines in file inFile.

```
numberOfLines = 0;
line = inFile.readLine();

// Assume at least one line
do
{
  numberOfLines++;
  line = inFile.readLine();
} while (line != null);
```

We may use the *do* statement to construct both count-controlled and event-controlled loops.

Looping: for

In contrast, the *for* statement is a looping construct designed specifically to simplify the implementation of count-controlled loops. The loop-control variable, the beginning value, the ending value, and the incrementation are explicitly part of the *for* heading itself. The following *for* loop reads and sums 10 values.

```
sum = 0;
for (counter = 1; counter <= 10; counter++)
{
  value = Integer.parseInt(dataFile.readLine());
  sum = sum + value;
}
```

counter, the loop-control variable, is initialized to 1. While counter is less than or equal to 10, the block of code is executed, and counter is incremented by 1. The loop is executed with counter equal to the initial value, the final value, and all the values in between. The second expression in the *for* heading is the assertion that controls the loop. If the assertion is false initially, the body of the loop is not executed. Here are two *for* headings and what they mean.

`for (counter = limit; counter != 0; counter--)`: Initialize `counter` to the value stored in `limit`; if `counter` is not equal to 0, execute the body of the loop; decrement `counter` by 1 and go back to the test. If `limit` contains the value 10, this *for* loop is identical to the previous one: It executes 10 times.

`for (int counter = 1; counter <= limit; counter++)`: Define an `int` variable `counter` and initialize it to 1. If `counter` is less than or equal to the value stored in `limit`, execute the body of the loop. Increment `counter` by 1. The scope of `counter` is the body of the loop, not the block in which the *for* statement is enclosed.

The *for* statement in Java is very flexible. Although designed to simplify count-controlled loops, it can be used for event-controlled loops. The first statement in the *for* header can be any statement—even the null statement. The second statement is a test that occurs at the beginning of the loop. The third statement is one that is executed at the end of the loop. However, we recommend that the *for* statement be used only for count-controlled loops. That is what *for* statements are designed for. Most other uses fall into the category of tricky code and should be avoided.

Loops constructed with the *while* statement and the *for* statement are called pretest loops because the expression is tested at the beginning of the loop before the body of the loop is executed the first time. Loops constructed with the *do* statement are called posttest loops because the expression is tested at the end of the loop.

Exception Handling

An exception is an unusual situation that occurs when the program is running. Although we usually think of an exception as being an error, it isn't necessarily so. It might be an unusual combination of circumstances within an application that requires special handling. Exception handling involves four stages: determining what constitutes an exception, naming the exception object, detecting the exception, and handling the exceptional situation. Let's look at each of these stages.

The first stage occurs before any program is written. During the design phase, all situations that might need special handling are examined and decisions are made on how to handle them. The Java system has already predefined a collection of errors such as trying to instantiate a file object with the name of a file that doesn't exist, dividing by zero, or trying to convert a string that contains letters to a number.

The second stage is deciding what to call the exception. The third stage is recognizing that the error has occurred, which is done somewhere in the program code. When the code detects an exceptional situation, it throws the exception determined in the second stage. Here are two examples:

```
throw new IOException;      // A predefined Java exception
throw new ExceptionClass(); // A class
```

where `IOException` is the name of a predefined system exception and `new ExceptionClass()` instantiates an object of a user-defined class `ExceptionClass`. Only objects of classes derived from `Throwable` can be thrown.

The last stage is "catching" the exception object and handling the situation. In this stage the code that is written to take care of the exception is executed. The code that detects the exception is enclosed in a *try* clause; the code to handle the situation is in an associated *catch* clause. Here is an example.

```
try
{
  dataFile = new PrintWriter(new FileWriter("data"));
}
catch (IOException newExcept)
{
  System.out.println("File data does not exist.");
}
```

If the file `data` cannot be found, the system throws an `IOException`. The parameter on the *catch* clause is of class `IOException`, so if the file cannot be found, the *catch* writes a message on `System.out`. There can be more than one *catch* clause associated with a *try* clause. The appropriate *catch* is chosen by matching the class of the thrown exception with the class of the *catch* parameter.

Java has a predefined class `Exception` that provides a field for an error message. Here is a class that extends `Exception`.

```
public class MyException extends Exception
{
  public MyException()                    // Default constructor
  {
    super();
  }
  public MyException(String message)  // Constructor w/string
  {
    super(message);
  }
}
```

If we define a *catch* clause that takes `MyException` as a parameter, the code can access the message using the `getMessage` method of class `Exception`, which is derived from class `Throwable`.

```
try
{
  // Code that can throw an exception
  throw new MyException("We have a problem");
  ...
}
catch (MyException newExcept)
{
  System.out.println(newExcept.getMessage());
}
```

The message "We have a problem" is written on `System.out`.

Laboratory 9: Prelab Assignment

Name _____ Date _____

Section _____

Read program `Loops` carefully and answer Exercises 1 and 2.

```java
// Program Loops demonstrates various looping structures.
import java.io.*;
public class Loops
{
  public static BufferedReader inData;
  public static void main(String[] args) throws IOException
  {
    inData = new BufferedReader(new FileReader("Loop.dat"));
    int  value;

    {// while loop
      int  counter = 1;
      int  sum = 0;
      while (counter <= 4)
      {
        value = Integer.parseInt(inData.readLine());
        sum = sum + value;
        counter++;
      }
      System.out.println(sum);
    }

    {// do loop
      int  counter = 1;
      int  sum = 0;
      do
      {
        value = Integer.parseInt(inData.readLine());
        sum = sum + value;
        counter++;
      } while (counter <= 4);
      System.out.println(sum);
    }

    {// for loop
      int  sum = 0;
      for (int counter = 1; counter <= 4; counter++)
      {
        value = Integer.parseInt(inData.readLine());
        sum = sum + value;
      }
      System.out.println(sum);
    }
  }
}
```

Exercise 1: If file `Loop.dat` contains the following values (one per line), what is printed?

10 20 30 40 10 20 30 40 10 20 30 40

Exercise 2: Which of these loops are pretest loops? Which are posttest loops?

Examine program `Switches` and answer Exercises 3 and 4.

```java
// Program Switches demonstrates the use of the Switch
//   statement.

import java.awt.*;
import java.awt.event.*;
import javax.swing.*;
public class Switches
{
  private static class ButtonListener
    implements ActionListener
  {
    public void actionPerformed(ActionEvent event)
    {
      char code;
      int answer;
      int one;
      int two;
      code = letter.getText().charAt(0);
      if (code != 'Q')
      {
        one = Integer.parseInt(first.getText());
        two = Integer.parseInt(second.getText());
        first.setText("");
        second.setText("");
        letter.setText("");
        switch (code)
        {
          case 'A' : answer = (one + two);
                     System.out.println(one  + " + "  + two
                       + " is "  + answer);
                     break;
          case 'S' : answer = (one - two);
                     System.out.println(one  + " - "
                     + two + " is " + answer);
                     break;
        }
      }
      else
      {
        outFrame.dispose();
```

```
        System.exit(0);
      }
    }
  }

  private static JFrame outFrame;
  private static JTextField letter;
  private static JTextField first;
  private static JTextField second;
  private static JButton enter;

  public static void main(String[] args)
  {
    Container outPane;

    // Set up frame
    outFrame = new JFrame();
    outFrame.setSize(600, 400);
    outFrame.setDefaultCloseOperation(JFrame.EXIT_ON_CLOSE);
    // Set up content pane
    outPane = outFrame.getContentPane();
    outPane.setLayout(new GridLayout(0, 2));

    // Set up labels
    JLabel prompt = new JLabel("Enter A for Addition;"
      + " S for subtraction;" + " Q for quit.");
    JLabel prompt2 = new JLabel("First integer number: ");
    JLabel prompt3 = new JLabel("Second integer number: ");
     // Set up input text fields
    letter = new JTextField(1);
    first = new JTextField(3);
    second = new JTextField(3);

    // Set up button
    enter = new JButton("Enter");
    ButtonListener listener = new ButtonListener();
    enter.addActionListener(listener);

    // Add items to pane
    outPane.add(prompt);
    outPane.add(letter);
    outPane.add(prompt2);
    outPane.add(first);
    outPane.add(prompt3);
    outPane.add(second);
    outPane.add(enter);

    outFrame.setVisible(true);
  }
}
```

Exercise 3: What is printed if the following values are entered?

```
A   5   -7
A  -5   -8
S   7    7
S   8   -8
Q
```

Exercise 4: What happens if the Q to quit is entered as a lower case letter?

Lesson 9-1: Check Prelab Exercises

Name _____ Date _____

Section _____

Exercise 1: Run program `Loops` and check your answers. Were your answers correct? If not, do you understand your mistakes?

Exercise 2: *while* loops and *for* loops are pretest loops; the loop body is not executed if the ending condition is true initially. *do* loops are posttest loops; their bodies are always executed at least once.

Exercise 3: Run program `Switches` to check your answers. Were your answers correct? If not, do you understand your mistakes?

Exercise 4: If a lowercase *Q* is entered, the first clause is executed. The screen freezes waiting for you to enter more values.

Lesson 9-2: Multi-Way Branching

Name _____ Date _____

Section _____

Exercise 1: Class `Switches` uses a combination of an *if* statement and a *switch*. Rewrite the button handler to use just a *switch* statement. Compile and rerun your program. Show your answer.

Exercise 2: As Prelab Exercise 4 demonstrated, program `Switches` is not very robust. Add the code necessary to allow the program to work properly with both lowercase and uppercase versions of the input letters. Run your program with the same data, but key the letters as lowercase.

Exercise 3: Program `Switches` is still not very robust. Add a default case that prints an error message and asks for the letter to be reentered. Test your program with the same data set, but add several letters that are not correct. Compile and run your program. Show your output.

Exercise 4: Program `Shell1` is the shell of a program that counts all the punctuation marks in a file.

```
// Program Shell1 counts punctuation marks in a file.
import java.io.*;
public class Shell1
{
  public static BufferedReader inFile;
  public static void main(String[] args)
    throws IOException, StringIndexOutOfBoundsException
  {
    String line;
    inFile = new BufferedReader(new FileReader("Shell1.dat"));
    char symbol;
    int  periodCt = 0;
    int  commaCt = 0;
    int  questionCt = 0;
    int  colonCt = 0;
    int  semicolonCt = 0;
    line = inFile.readLine();
    while (line != null)                    // Loop til end of data
    {
```

```
        for (int count = 0; count < line.length(); count++)
        { // Loop til end of line
          symbol = line.charAt(count);
            /* FILL IN */
        }
        line = inFile.readLine();
      }
    }
}
```

Fill in the missing code and run your program.

Number of periods: _____   Number of commas: _____
Number of question marks: _____   Number of colons: _____
Number of semicolons: _____

Exercise 5: Add the code necessary for program She111 to count blanks as well. How many blanks are there in file she111.dat? If you did not get 11, go back and check your program.

Lesson 9-3: Additional Control Structures

Name _____ Date _____

Section _____

Use program Looping for Exercises 1, 2, and 3. This program reads and sums exactly 10 integers and then reads and sums integers until a negative value is read.

```java
// Program Looping uses a count-controlled loop to read and
//  sum 10 integer values and an event-controlled loop to
//  read and sum values until a negative value is found.
//  The data is on file Looping.dat

import java.io.*;
public class Looping
{
  public static BufferedReader inData;
  public static void main(String[] args) throws IOException
  {
    inData = new BufferedReader(
      new FileReader("Looping.dat"));
    int   value;
    int   counter;
    int   sum;

    counter = 1;
    sum = 0;
    while (counter <= 10)
    {// Ten values read and summed
      value = Integer.parseInt(inData.readLine());
      sum = sum + value;
      counter++;
    }
    System.out.println("The first sum is "  + sum);

    value = Integer.parseInt(inData.readLine());
    sum = 0;
    while (value >= 0)
    {// Values are read and summed until a negative is read
      sum = sum + value;
      value = Integer.parseInt(inData.readLine());
    }
    System.out.println("The second sum is "  + sum);
  }
}
```

Exercise 1: Compile and run program `Looping`.

First sum is _____.

Second sum is _____.

Exercise 2: Program `Looping` contains two loops implemented with *while* statements. Rewrite program `Looping`, replacing the *while* statements with *do* statements.

First sum is _____.

Second sum is _____.

Exercise 3: Can program `Looping` be rewritten using a *for* statement for each loop? Explain.

Rewrite program `Looping` using a *for* statement to implement the count-controlled loop.

First sum is _____.

Second sum is _____.

Exercise 4: Rerun your program using data file `Looping.d2`. Describe what happens.

If an error condition was generated, correct your program and rerun the program.

First sum is _____.

Second sum is _____.

Lesson 9-4: Exception Handling

Name _____ Date _____

Section _____

Exercise 1: In Exercise 2 in Lesson 9-2, we pointed out that class `Switches` was not very robust. You were asked in Exercise 3 to use the default case in the *switch* statement to handle the case of incorrect input data. Rewrite this solution so that an object of an exception class is thrown on the default case. Compile and run your solution. Compare your output with the output in Exercise 3. Were they the same?

Exercise 2: Go through the classes in this lesson and count how many of them could throw an `IOException`. How many are there?

Exercise 3: For each of the classes in Exercise 3 that could throw an `IOException`, write the code to catch the exception and print an appropriate message on `System.out`. Handle the exception without stopping execution if possible.

Lesson 9-5: Debugging

Name _____ Date _____

Section _____

Exercise 1: Program Bugs is supposed to sum the first ten values on a file and the second ten values on a file. The second ten values are a duplicate of the first ten, so the answers should be the same. The program checks to be sure that the file has been found and halts execution if the file is not found. Program Bugs compiles, says that the file cannot be found, but then crashes. Can you find the problem? Describe it.

Exercise 2: Correct the problem and rerun the program. The file cannot be found, but now the program halts correctly. Correct the name of the file and rerun the program.

Exercise 3: What—the program crashes again? Back to the drawing board. Describe the next error you find. Correct the program and run it again.

Exercise 4: Now you are getting output, but the answer is wrong for the second sum. When you find this last error, describe it, correct it, and rerun the program. What are the correct totals?

Postlab Activities

Exercise 1: Write a design and a program to analyze a sample of text. Count the instances of the following categories of symbols:

- Uppercase letters
- Lowercase letters
- Digits
- End-of-sentence markers (periods, exclamation points, and question marks)
- Intra-sentence markers (commas, semicolons, and colons)
- Blanks
- All other symbols

Use a *switch* statement in your processing.

After collecting these statistics, use them to approximate the following statistics:

- Average word length
- Average sentence length

Exercise 2: Design and implement a test plan for the program in Exercise 1.

Exercise 3: Scoring a tennis game is different from scoring any other game. The following table shows how a tennis game is scored. The score is always given with the server's score first. In this table, Player 1 is the server.

Score	Player 1 Wins Point	Player 2 Wins Point
0/0	15/0	0/15
0/15	15/15	0/30
0/30	15/30	0/40
0/40	15/40	game
15/0	30/0	15/15
15/15	30/15	15/30
15/30	30/30	15/40
15/40	30/40	game
30/0	40/0	30/15
30/15	40/15	30/30
30/30	40/30	30/40
30/40	<u>30/30</u>	game
40/0	game	40/15
40/15	game	40/30
40/30	game	<u>30/30</u>

The two underlined scores (30/30) should actually be 40/40, but in tennis you have to win by 2 points, so 40/40 behaves like 30/30. (See what we mean about being strange?) Write a function that takes two scores and the player who won the point as input and returns the new scores. This function is more complex than any you have done so far. Treat it like a complete program. Begin with a top-down design that outlines your solution. There are 15 possibilities, but some can be combined. You must use at least one *switch* statement in your program.

Exercise 4: Write a test plan for the function written for Exercise 3. Implement your test plan.

One–Dimensional Arrays

Objectives

- ■ To be able to declare and instantiate a one-dimensional array variable.

- ■ To be able to manipulate a one-dimensional array variable.

- ■ To be able to apply subarray processing.

- ■ To be able to use an array where the indexes have semantic content.

Laboratory 10: Assignment Cover Sheet

Name _____ Date _____

Section _____

Fill in the following table showing which exercises have been assigned for each lesson and check what you are to submit: (1) lab sheets, (2) listings of output files, and/or (3) listings of code. Your instructor or teaching assistant (TA) can use the Completed column for grading purposes.

Activities	Assigned: Check or list exercise numbers	Submit (1) (2) (3)			Completed
Prelab					
Review					
Prelab Assignment					
Inlab					
Lesson 10-1: Check Prelab Exercises					
Lesson 10-2: One-Dimensional Arrays with `int` Indexes					
Lesson 10-3: One-Dimensional Arrays with `char` Indexes					
Lesson 10-4: One-Dimensional Arrays of Objects					
Lesson 10-5: Test Plan					
Postlab					

Prelab Activities

Review

Recall that Java has two kinds of data types: primitive and reference. We have examined all of the primitive types and the class. There are two data types left to examine: the `array` and the `interface`. Arrays come in several varieties; in this chapter we look at one-dimensional arrays, and in Laboratory 12 we look at multidimensional arrays. In Laboratory 11 we look at interfaces.

One-Dimensional Arrays

A *one-dimensional array* is a structured data type in which a collection of places is given a name and the individual places are accessed by their position within the collection. There are two types associated with the array data type: the type of the items to be stored in the individual places in the structure and the type of the index used to specify the individual places within the structure. In Java, the type of the index must be `byte`, `char`, `short`, or `int`.

Declaring and Instantiating an Array

Arrays are reference types, so the array variable is declared and then the array itself is instantiated and the address is stored in the array variable. Look at the following code fragment.

```
final int MAX_ITEMS = 100;        // Define a constant
int[]  dataValues;                // Declare an array variable
dataValues = new int[MAX_ITEMS];  // Instantiate the array
int  index;
```

`dataValues` is an array variable; it is declared by putting a pair of brackets next to the type. When `dataValues` is instantiated, an integer expression in brackets tells the system how many components the array should have. In this case `dataValues` contains 100 `int` variables. If the individual elements are primitive types, they are set to the default value for the type. Therefore, each of the 100 variables in `dataValues` is set to 0.

Java provides an alternative way to declare and instantiate an array. This construct is called an *initializer*.

```
double[] cost = {12.33, 33.66, 99.95, 9.99};
```

`cost` is an array made up of four `double` values. The first is `12.33`, the second is `33.66`, the third is `99.95`, and the fourth is `9.99`. An initializer allows you to combine instantiating the array and storing values.

Accessing Array Elements

How do we access the individual elements? Giving the name of the array variable followed by its position (index) in the collection accesses an individual variable within the array. For example, `dataValues[0]` accesses the first variable in the collection, `dataValues[1]` accesses the second variable in the collection, and `dataValues[MAX_ITEMS-1]` accesses the last variable in the collection. Notice that the items in the collection are indexed from zero through the number in the collection minus one. The following code segment would set each of the variables in the array variable `dataValues` to its own index position.

```
for (index = 0; index < MAX_ITEMS; index++)
  dataValues[index] = index;
```

The following code segment reads in ten values from file `inFile` and writes them out on `System.out`.

```
for (index = 0; index < 10; index++)
{
  dataValues[index] =
    Integer.parseInt(inFile.readLine());
  System.out.print(" " + dataValues[index]);
}
```

The following code segment writes the values in `cost` on file `outFile`.

```
for (index = 0; index < 4; index++)
  outFile.println("$" + cost[index]);
```

What happens if the less-than operator were incorrectly keyed as less-than-or-equal? There are only four places in the array, so the last access would be to `cost[4]`, which doesn't exist. This error is called an *out-of-bounds* error. If this error occurs in a program an `ArrayIndexOutOfBoundsException` is thrown. Fortunately, Java provides a way to protect against this error. With each array that is instantiated, a public instance field called `length` is defined. If all array accesses are checked against `length`, then this exception will not be thrown.

```
for (index = 0; index < cost.length; index++)
  outFile.println("$" + cost[index];
```

Aggregate Array Operations

One array may be assigned to another, and two arrays may be compared for equality. However, you might be surprised at the results. Arrays are reference types, so array assignment is a shallow assignment. The pointer to the array is copied rather than the array itself. The same is true of array comparisons. The comparison compares addresses rather than the contents of the places pointed to.

If a problem needs a deep array copy or comparison, the code must be written to perform these operations element by element.

Arrays of Objects

The types of the components of an array are not limited to primitive types; they can be classes as well. For example, the following code segment declares, instantiates, and reads values into an array of strings. Assume `inFile` has been instantiated.

```
String[] myLyrics;
myLyrics = new String[10];
String oneLine;
oneLine = inFile.readLine();
int index = 0;
while (oneLine != null && index < myLyrics.length)
{
  myLyrics[index] = oneLine;
  index++;
  oneLine = inFile.readLine();
}
```

This example demonstrates the fact that there are two important pieces of information associated with an array. The first is the number of components defined, and the second is the number of components that have valid data stored in them. When an array of reference types is instantiated, each component is set to `null`. However, in our example only `index` components have valid strings stored in them. Java provides the `length` field to tell us the number of components, but we must keep track of the number of actual data values stored into the array.

To print out the valid strings in the array, we must use `index` to control the loop, not `myLyrics.length`.

```
for (int counter = 0; counter < index; counter++)
  System.out.println(myLyrics[counter]);
```

This type of process is often called *subarray* processing because only part of the array is being processed.

Arrays as Parameters

Arrays may be parameters just like any other type or class. Because they are reference types, a reference to the argument is passed to the method. Array components can be passed as arguments to methods if the parameter type or class is the same as the component type or class.

Indexes with Semantic Content

There are applications where the array indexes have meaning outside of just numbering the places in the array. For example, students might be assigned seat numbers from 0 to the number of seats minus one in alphabetic order. When the student names are read in alphabetic order and stored in the next place in the array, the index of where a name is stored is the same as the seat number. We say that this index has semantic content.

Laboratory 10: Prelab Assignment

Name _____ Date _____

Section _____

Exercise 1: Read program `Arrays` carefully.

```java
// Program Arrays manipulates values in an array.

public class Arrays
{
  public static void main(String[] args)
  {
    final int MAX_ARRAY = 5;
    int[]  numbers;
    numbers = new int[MAX_ARRAY];
    int  index;
    int  sum;

    // Stored values in the array.
    for (index = 0; index < numbers.length; index++)
      numbers[index] = index * index;

    // The values in the array are summed.
    sum = 0;
    for (index = 0; index < MAX_ARRAY; index++)
      sum = sum + numbers[index];
    System.out.println("Sum is "  + sum);
  }
}
```

Describe what is written on the screen.

Exercise 2: What would happen if the *for* loop headings were changed as follows?

```java
for (index = 0; index <= MAX_ARRAY; index++)
```

Lesson 10-1: Check Prelab Exercises

Name _____ Date _____

Section _____

Exercise 1: Run program Arrays to check your answer. Was your answer correct? If not, do you understand what you did wrong?

Exercise 2: An ArrayIndexOutOfBoundsException is thrown.

Lesson 10-2: One-Dimensional Arrays with `int` Indexes

Name _____ Date _____

Section _____

This lesson uses the following program shell.

```
// Program Reverse reads numbers into an array
//   and prints them out in reverse order.

import java.io.*;
public class Reverse
{
  public static void main(String[] args) throws IOException
  {
    final int MAX = 10;
    BufferedReader inFile =
      new BufferedReader(new FileReader("reverse.dat"));
    int[]  numbers;
    numbers = new int[MAX];

    int  value;
    int  index;
    for (index = 0; index < numbers.length; index++)
    {
      // FILL IN Code to read value
      // FILL IN Code to store value into numbers
    }

    for (index = MAX - 1; index >= 0; index--)
      // FILL IN Code to write numbers on the screen
  }
}
```

Exercise 1: Complete the missing code in program `Reverse` and run it. What is printed on the screen?

Exercise 2: Exercise 1 asked you to fill in the body of the first *for* loop with two statements. Replace these two statements with a single statement and rerun your program; your answer should be the same. If it is not, correct your code and rerun the program. Describe any problems that you had.

Exercise 3: Extend the program in Exercise 2 to print the sum of the values stored in numbers. What is the sum?

Lesson 10–3: One-Dimensional Arrays with `char` Indexes

Name _____ Date _____

Section _____

This lesson uses program `Text`.

```
// Program Text counts the occurrence of all characters
//  in a text file
import java.io.*;
public class TextAns
{
  public static void main(String[] args) throws IOException
  {
    int[] charCount;
    charCount = new int[256]; // Contains character counts
    char[] lineArray;

    int index;
    String line;
    BufferedReader inFile;
    inFile = new BufferedReader(new FileReader("text.dat"));

    line = inFile.readLine();

    while (/* TO BE FILLED IN: Exercise 1 */)
    {
      /* TO BE FILLED IN: Exercise 2 */
      // Convert line to array of char
      lineArray = line.toCharArray();
    }
    for (index = 0; index < charCount.length; index++)
    {
      /* TO BE FILLED IN: Exercise 3 */
    }
  }
}
```

Exercise 1: Complete the expression on the first *while* loop so that it continues until there is no more data.

Exercise 2: Complete the body of the first loop. Use each character as an index into the array `charCount`; this slot is where a frequency of the number of times that character has been seen is kept.

Exercise 3: Complete the body of the second loop so that each character that appears in the text is printed with its frequency of occurrence. Fill in the frequency of the following characters.

blanks   _____   a   _____

i   _____   I   _____

k   _____   Z   _____

Exercise 4: Alter the program so that it counts uppercase letters and lowercase letters together. Compile and run your program.

Exercise 5: There was one count (668) for which there is no character printed. Can you hypothesize what this count represents?

Exercise 6: This problem is another example of array indexes with semantic content. Explain.

Lesson 10–4: One-Dimensional Arrays of Objects

Name _____   Date _____

Section _____

Use classes `ImportantDate` and `Shell` for this lesson.

```
import date.*;
public class ImportantDate
{
  Date date;
  String reason;
  /* TO BE FILLED IN: Exercise 1 */
}

import java.io.*;
public class Shell
{
  public static void main(String[] args)
  {
    ImportantDates[] myDates;
    myDates = new ImportantDates[10];
    /* TO BE FILLED IN: Exercise 2 */
  }
}
```

Exercise 1: Complete the definition of class `ImportantDate`. Class `Date` can be found in Lesson 7-2, Exercise 1.

Exercise 2: Class `Shell` should create an array of dates that are important to you. Write the code to read the information from a file, create an object of class `ImportantDate`, store the object in the array `myDates`, and print the information.

Exercise 3: Create a data file with information on 5 important dates in your life. Compile and run the program from Exercise 2 using your file of dates. Show your output.

Lesson 10-5: Test Plan

Name _____ Date _____

Section _____

Exercise 1: Design a test plan for the program in Lesson 10-3. Use another page if necessary.

Reason for Test Case	Input Values	Expected Output	Observed Output

Exercise 2: Implement the test plan designed in Exercise 1. You may show the results in the chart in Exercise 1.

Postlab Activities

Exercise 1: Write a program to grade a set of true/false tests. There are 15 true/false questions. True is represented by 1, and false is represented by 0. The key to the quiz is on file `Quiz.dat` followed by the student responses. Each student's name (maximum of 15 characters) immediately follows the student's last answer. For each student write out the name followed by the number answered correctly and the number missed.

Exercise 2: An organization that your little cousin belongs to is selling low-fat cookies. If your cousin's class sells more cookies than any other class, the teacher has promised to take the whole class on a picnic. Of course, your cousin volunteered you to keep track of all the sales and determine the winner.

Each class has an identification number. Each sales slip has the class identification number and the number of boxes sold. You decide to create two arrays: one to hold the identification numbers and one to record the number of boxes sold. The identification numbers range from 1 through 10. Here is a sample of the data.

ID Number	Boxes Sold
3	23
4	1
2	13
2	7
4	5
1	6
10	16
.	.
.	.

The first time an identification number is read, store it in the next free slot in the array of identification numbers and initialize the corresponding position in the array of boxes sold to the number sold on the sales slip. Each subsequent time an identification number is read, add the number of boxes sold to the corresponding position in the array of boxes sold. You may assume that each class sold at least one box of cookies—the homeroom mothers had to buy one.

When there are no more sales slips, scan the array of boxes sold for the largest value. The identification number in the corresponding position in the array of identification numbers is the class that wins.

Write your program and run it using data file `Boxes.dat`. Which class won and how many boxes of cookies did they sell?

Exercise 3: In Exercise 2, the class identification numbers range from 1 through 10. If they ranged from 0 through 9, the identification number could be used as an index into the array of boxes sold. Using this scheme, you need only one array to hold the boxes sold. Rewrite your program implementing this scheme. You can use the same data file by always subtracting one from the identification number on input and adding one to the identification number on output. Run your program using `Boxes.dat`. You should get the same results as in Exercise 2. Did you?

Exercise 4: Write test plans for Exercises 2 and 3. Can these test plans be the same, or must they be different? Explain.

Exercise 5: If an index has meaning beyond simply indicating the place in the collection, we say that it has *semantic content*. Exercise 3 is an example of processing in which the array indexes have semantic content. Explain.

Array-Based Lists

- To be able to define the operations in a list.

- To be able to implement the operations on an unsorted list.

- To be able to implement the operations on a sorted list.

- To be able to define and implement an abstract class.

- To be able to implement the `Comparable` interface.

Laboratory 11: Assignment Cover Sheet

Name _____ Date _____

Section _____

Fill in the following table showing which exercises have been assigned for each lesson and check what you are to submit: (1) lab sheets, (2) listings of output files, and/or (3) listings of code. Your instructor or teaching assistant (TA) can use the Completed column for grading purposes.

Activities	Assigned: Check or list exercise numbers	Submit (1) (2) (3)			Completed
Prelab					
Review					
Prelab Assignment					
Inlab					
Lesson 11-1: Check Prelab Exercises					
Lesson 11-2: Unsorted List Operations					
Lesson 11-3: Sorted List Operations					
Lesson 11-4: Abstract Classes					
Postlab					

Prelab Activities

Review

An array gives a name to a collection of data values and lets us access individual items by their position within the collection. Arrays are ideal structures to represent *lists* of items.

Lists

Lists occur as naturally in programming as they do in real life. We manipulate guest lists, grocery lists, class lists, things-to-do lists. . . . The list of lists is endless. Three properties characterize lists: The items are homogeneous, the items are linear, and lists have varying length. By linear we mean that each item except the first has a unique component that comes before it and each item except the last has a unique component that comes after it. For example, if there are at least three items in a list, the second item comes after the first and before the third.

A set of operations that manipulates a list must include at least one operation for initializing a list, putting an item on a list, removing an item from a list, searching for an item in a list, determining if a list is empty, and displaying the items in a list.

Array-Based Lists

An array is the structure that is often used to represent items in a list. The first item in the list is stored in the first place in the array, the second item in the list is stored in the second place in the array, and so on. The number of positions in an array is fixed when the array is instantiated, but the number of items in a list varies as a program executes. Therefore, when an array is used to implement a list, there must be a *length* parameter associated with the list. Let's examine a simple general class declaration that defines a length and an array of integer items. (The comments must be replaced with actual values before the declarations can be used.)

```java
public class List
{
  final int MAX_LENGTH = 20;
  int[] list;
  int  length;
  public List()
  {
    list = new int[MAX_LENGTH];
    length = 0;
  }
  // Methods to manipulate the list
  ...
}
```

The second statement declares an `int` array; the next statement declares an `int` variable. The constructor instantiates the array, using a constant. The constructor also sets `length` to 0.

Distinction between the Array and the List

At the logical level, the length of an empty list is zero. As each successive item is entered into the list, the item is stored into the array variable at the position indexed by `length`, and `length` is incremented. All processing of the logical list is done from the zeroth position in the array variable `list` through the `length-1` position.

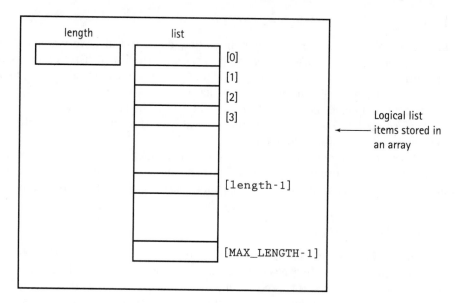

Sorted and Unsorted Lists

Lists can be categorized into two classes: sorted and unsorted. In an unsorted list, the component that comes before or after an item has no semantic relationship with it. In a sorted list, the items are arranged in such a way that the component that comes before or after an item has a semantic relationship with that item. For example, a grade list can be a random list of numbers or sorted by value. The following diagrams show an unsorted list of grades and a sorted list of grades.

Unsorted List

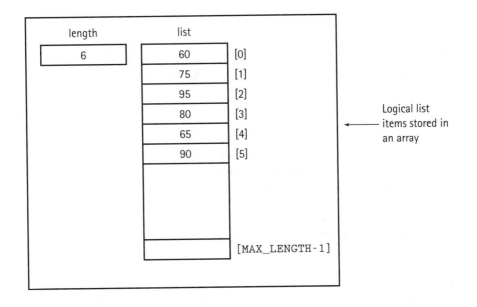

Logical list items stored in an array

Sorted List

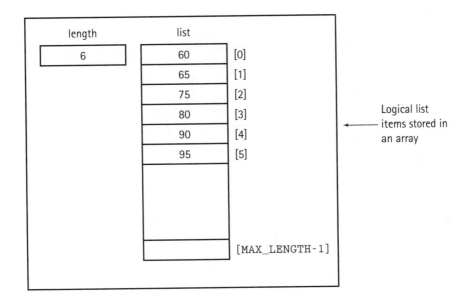

Logical list items stored in an array

We have used the identifier `length` in our discussion to mean the number of items in the list because this is the term used in the literature. However, Java automatically appends a field named `length` to each array. Java is not confused between `List.length` and `list.length`. The first is the `length` field defined in class `List`; the second is the `length` field associated with the array `list`. However, these fields mean very different things: One is the number of data items stored into an array, and the other is the number of cells in the array.

The compiler doesn't get confused, but a human reader of the code would probably have a hard time keeping track of the ambiguity of the two identifiers. Therefore, we suggest that another term be used for the number of items in the list. `numItems` would be a good choice.

List Algorithms

In the following algorithms, we use *list* and *length* in their logical meaning. That is, they are not program variables but logical entities.

Storing an item in an unsorted list: The item is stored in the length position and length is incremented.

Inserting an item in a sorted list: Find the position where the item should be inserted (use one of the sorted searches below), move the items in the array from that point to the end down one position, store the item, and increment the length.

Linear searching in an unsorted list: To search for an item in an unsorted list, loop through the items in the list examining each one until you find the item you are searching for or you run out of items to examine.

Linear searching in a sorted list: If the list items are sorted, the loop can terminate when the item is found or when the place where the item would be if it were in the list is passed. For example, if you are searching for the grade 70, you can terminate the search when the value 75 is encountered.

Binary searching: A binary search is only possible if the list is sorted. Rather than looking for the item starting at the beginning of the list and moving forward, you begin at the middle in a binary search. If the item for which you are searching is less than the item in the middle, continue searching between the beginning of the list and the middle. If the item for which you are searching is greater than the item in the middle, continue searching between the middle and the end of the list. If the middle item is equal to the one for which you are searching, the search stops. The process continues with each comparison cutting in half the portion of the list left to be searched. The process stops when the item is found or when the portion of the list left to be searched is empty.

Sorting: Sorting a list converts it from unsorted to sorted. One algorithm for doing so is as follows. Define the current item to be the first in the list (the value in the zeroth position). Find the minimum value in the rest of the part of the list from the current position to the end and exchange it with the value in the current position. Increment the current position and repeat the process. When the current position is equal to the length minus two, the process stops and the list is sorted.

Abstract Classes

In Laboratory 7, we said that a class marked `abstract` is one that is incomplete, that there are one or more class methods that have not been defined. An undefined method is one that is marked `abstract` and just has the signature followed by a semicolon instead of a method body. An abstract list class might have all the methods defined except for the method that searches for an item. Then one derived class could implement the method using a linear search and another derived class could implement the method using a binary search.

Comparable Interface

When we defined a button listener class in Laboratory 8, we said that the class had to follow a strict pattern.

```
private static class MyListener implements ActionListener
{
  public void actionPerformed(ActionEvent event)
  {
    // Here is where we specify what to do when the button is
    //  pressed
  }
}
```

The pattern that had to be followed is spelled out in the `ActionListener` interface. The keyword `implements` says that the class being defined must implement the instance methods specified in the interface.

An `interface` is the last of the Java types. All the methods defined in an interface are `public` and `abstract`, even if the modifiers are omitted. Any class that implements an interface must implement all of the methods.

The `Comparable` interface has one method, `compareTo`. This method compares two objects and returns an integer that determines the ordering of the two objects. If the object to which the method is applied comes first, a negative number is returned. If the objects are the same, zero is returned. If the parameter comes before the object, a positive number is returned. Does this sound familiar? It should. The `String` class implements the `Comparable` interface; you have been using `compareTo` with strings for some time now.

Laboratory 11: Prelab Assignment

Name _____ Date _____

Section _____

Read the following code carefully.

```java
import java.io.*;
public class FloatList
{
  public void getList(BufferedReader inFile)
    throws IOException
  {
    float  item;
    String data;
    data  = inFile.readLine();
    while (data != null)
    {
      values[numItems] = Float.parseFloat(data);
      numItems++;
      data = inFile.readLine();
    }
  }

  public void PrintList()
  {
    int  index;

    for (index = 0; index < numItems; index++)
      System.out.println(values[index]);
  }

  public FloatList(int maxItems)
  {
    numItems = 0;
    values = new float[maxItems];
  }
  private int numItems;
  private float[] values;
}
import java.io.*;
public class UseList
{
  public static BufferedReader inFile;
  public static void main(String[] args) throws IOException
  {
    inFile = new BufferedReader(new FileReader("real.dat"));
    FloatList  list;
    list = new FloatList(50);
```

```
        list.getList(inFile);
        list.printList();
        inFile.close();
    }
}
```

Exercise 1: Document the class heading for `FloatList`.

Exercise 2: Document the methods of `FloatList`.

Exercise 3: Document class `UseList`.

Lesson 11-1: Check Prelab Exercises

Name _____ Date _____

Section _____

In order to be able to write documentation, you must thoroughly understand the code. Run program `FloatList`. What were the last four values printed?

The version of program `FloatList` on the disk is documented.

Exercise 1: Check the class documentation for class `FloatList`. Did you understand what the program was doing? If not, describe what you did not understand.

Exercise 2: Check the documentation for the methods of `FloatList`. Did you understand what the methods were doing? If not, describe what you did not understand.

Exercise 3: Check the documentation for `UseList`. Did you understand how the methods were being implemented? If not, describe what you did not understand.

Lesson 11-2: Unsorted List Operations

Name _____   Date _____

Section _____

Use the following shell `List` for Exercises 1 through 6. Read the documentation on the member function declarations carefully. The documentation is in terms of preconditions (what the method assumes to be true) and postconditions (what the method promises to be true on exit).

```
public class List
{
  // Methods
  public void store(int item)
  // Pre:  The list is not full
  // Post: item is in the list
  public void printList()
  // Post: If the list is not empty, the elements are
  //       printed on the screen; otherwise "The list
  //       is empty" is printed on the screen
  public int length()
  // Post: return value is the number of items in the list
  public boolean isEmpty()
  // Post: returns true if list is empty; false otherwise
  public boolean isFull()
  // Post: returns true if there is no more room in the
  //       list; false otherwise
  public List(int maxItems)
  // Constructor
  // Post: Empty list is created with maxItems cells

  // Data fields
  private  int length;
  private  int[] values;
}
```

Exercise 1: Write the bodies of the methods. There is nothing in the documentation for the member functions that indicates order. Therefore, implement `store` by putting each new value in the next space in the array.

Exercise 2: Write a driver program that reads values from file `int.dat`, stores them in the list, and prints them on the screen. What are the last four values in the file?

Exercise 3: Add a method `isThere` to class `List` that returns `true` if its parameter is in the list and `false` otherwise.

Exercise 4: Add a method `removeItem` that removes a value from the list. The precondition is that the value is in the list.

Exercise 5: Add a method `writeList` that writes the values in the list to a file passed as a parameter.

Exercise 6: Write a test driver that tests the member functions added in Exercises 3 through 5 using the data on file `int.dat`. Have your driver complete the following activities:

- Read and store the values into the list.
- Print the values to a file.
- Search for a value that is there (10) and print the results.
- Search for a value that is not there (5) and print the results.
- Delete a value (10) and print the list with the value removed.

Lesson 11-3: Sorted List Operations

Name _____   Date _____

Section _____

Use the following shell SList for Exercises 1 through 7. Read the documentation on the member function declarations carefully.

```
public class SList
{
  // Methods
  public void insert(int item)
  // Pre:  The list is not full
  // Post: item is in the list; the items are in sorted order
  public void printList()
  // Post: If the list is not empty, the elements are
  //       printed on the screen; otherwise "The list
  //       is empty" is printed on the screen
  public int length()
  // Post: return value is the number of items in the list
  public boolean isEmpty()
  // Post: returns true if list is empty; false otherwise
  public boolean isFull()
  // Post: returns true if there is no more room in the
  //       list; false otherwise
  public SList(int maxItems)
  // Constructor
  // Post: Empty list is created with maxItems cells

  // Data fields
  private  int length;
  private  int[] values;
}
```

Exercise 1: Write the definitions for the member functions.

Exercise 2: Write a driver program that reads values from file int.dat, stores them in the list, and prints them on the screen. Be sure that your driver adheres to the preconditions on the member functions. What are the last four values in the file?

Exercise 3: Add a method isThere to class SList that returns true if its parameter is in the list and false otherwise.

Exercise 4: Add a method `removeItem` that removes a value from the list. The precondition is that the value is in the list.

Exercise 5: Add a method `writeList` that writes the values in the list to a file passed as a parameter.

Exercise 6: Write a test driver that tests the member functions added in Exercises 3 through 5 using the data on file `int.dat`. Have your driver complete the following activities:

- Read and store the values into the list.
- Print the values to a file.
- Search for a value that is there (10) and print the results.
- Search for a value that is not there (5) and print the results.
- Delete a value (10) and print the list with the value removed.

Exercise 7: Were you able to use any method implementation you wrote in Lesson 11-2 for Exercises 1 through 6? Explain.

Lesson 11-4: Abstract Classes

Name _____ Date _____

Section _____

Exercise 1: Create an abstract class named `AbstractList` with all the methods defined in Lesson 3.

Exercise 2: Derive class `List` from `AbstractList`. Compile and run your driver program on the same data you used in Lesson 3. Your answers should be the same.

Exercise 3: Derive class `SList` from `AbstractList`. `List` used `store` for the method that put a value into the list; `SList` used `insert`. For your derived class, use the identifier `store`. Compile and run your driver program on the same data you used in Lesson 4. Your answers should be the same.

Exercise 4: Which of the methods had to be abstract and which could be concrete? Explain.

Exercise 5: Rewrite `AbstractList` using `Comparable` as the class of the items on the list.

Exercise 6: Derive `SList` from `AbstractList` where the items on the list are of class `String`. Compile and run your driver program using file `strings.dat`. What are the last two values printed?

Postlab Activities

Exercise 1: In Postlab Exercise 2 in Laboratory 10, you wrote a program to keep track of low-fat cookie sales for your cousin. Rewrite the program using the sorted list operations you wrote for this laboratory. Can you keep both lists sorted? Can you keep one or the other sorted but not both? Write a justification for the data structures you use.

Exercise 2: Write and implement a test plan for your program in Exercise 1.

Exercise 3: A clothing manufacturer wants to keep track of how many copies of each item are sold over a period of a week. The information on the sales slip includes the item identification number, the number of copies sold, the unit price, and the total amount of the sale. How is the problem similar to judging a cookie contest (Postlab Exercise 2, Laboratory 10)? How is the problem different? What changes would be necessary if the manufacturer asked you to include a total sales figure at the end of the week?

Exercise 4: Write a program to implement the problem described in Exercise 3, including the total sales figure.

Exercise 5: Postlab Exercises 4 and 5 in Laboratory 5 were simulations of a children's game to determine who would be "it." Rewrite your solution to Exercise 4 in Laboratory 5 using a list of children's names. Print out the name of the child who is it rather than the position that the child occupies in the original grouping.

Exercise 6: Rewrite your solution to Exercise 5 using the altered form described in Postlab Exercise 5 in Laboratory 5.

Multidimensional Arrays

Objectives

- To be able to define a two-dimensional array.

- To be able to read, store, and print values in a table (two-dimensional array object).

- To be able to find the minimum value and the maximum value in a table.

- To be able to sum the individual rows of a table.

Laboratory 12: Assignment Cover Sheet

Name _____ Date _____

Section _____

Fill in the following table showing which exercises have been assigned for each lesson and check what you are to submit: (1) lab sheets, (2) listings of output files, and/or (3) listings of code. Your instructor or teaching assistant (TA) can use the Completed column for grading purposes.

Activities	Assigned: Check or list exercise numbers	Submit (1) (2) (3)			Completed
Prelab					
Review					
Prelab Assignment					
Inlab					
Lesson 12-1: Check Prelab Exercises					
Lesson 12-2: Two-Dimensional Arrays					
Lesson 12-3: Multidimensional Arrays					
Lesson 12-4: Debugging					
Postlab					

Prelab Activities

Review

A *two-dimensional array* is a collection of components of the same type that is structured in two dimensions. Individual components are accessed by their position within each dimension. Three types are associated with a two-dimensional array object: the type of the items to be stored in the individual places in the structure, the type of the index for the first dimension, and the type of the index for the second dimension. In Java, the type of both dimensions must be `byte`, `char`, `short`, or `int`.

Declaring and Instantiating a Two-Dimensional Array

Declaring and instantiating a two-dimensional array is a logical extension of declaring and instantiating a one-dimensional array.

```
int[][] twoDArray;
twoDArray = new int[10][5];
```

twoDArray is an array variable that has 10 rows and 5 columns. Each row and column entry is of type `int`. The instantiating process sets each value to 0, the default value for the `int` data type. The following code fragment sets all the entries in `twoDArray` to minus 1.

```
for (int column = 0; column < 5; column++)
  for(int row = 0; row < 10; row++)
    twoDArray[row][column] = -1;
```

Java actually views two-dimensional arrays as a one-dimensional array of references to one-dimensional arrays. Hence, each row in a two-dimensional array is a one-dimensional array with a `length` field. In this example, `twoDArray.length` is the number of rows in the array and `twoDArray[0].length` gives the number of components in the first row of the array. Because of this structure, Java allows the length of the rows to be different. If the rows do have different lengths, the array is called a *ragged* array.

Table Processing

Just as a one-dimensional array object is the structure used to represent items in a list, a two-dimensional array object is the structure that is often used to represent items in a *table*. The number of rows and columns in the two-dimensional array is fixed when the array is instantiated. The number of rows and columns in the table can vary as the program executes. Therefore, each dimension should have a length parameter associated with it that contains the number of rows or columns actually used.

Processing a table requires two loops: one for the rows and one for the columns. If the outer loop is the index for the column, the table is processed by column. If the outer loop is the index for the row, the table is processed by row. The loop shown previously processes `twoDArray` by columns.

Multidimensional Arrays

You have seen one-dimensional and two-dimensional arrays. In Java, arrays may have any number of dimensions. To process every item in a one-dimensional array, you need one loop. To process every item in a two-dimensional array, you need two loops. The pattern continues to any number of dimensions. To process every item in an *n*-dimensional array, you need *n* loops.

Laboratory 12: Prelab Assignment

Name _____ Date _____

Section _____

Exercise 1: What does the following code segment print if MAX_ROWS is 10 and MAX_COLS is 10? Fill in the table shown below the code.

```
rowsUsed = 5;
colsUsed = 5;
int row;
int column;

for (column = 0; column < MAX_COLS; column++)
  for (row = 0; row < MAX_ROWS; row++)
    table[row][column] = '*';

for (row = rowsUsed; row < MAX_ROWS; row++)
  for (column = colsUsed; column < MAX_COLS; column++)
    table[row][column] = '+';

for (column = 0; column < colsUsed; column++)
  for (row = 0; row < rowsUsed; row++)
    table[row][column] = '_';
```

Exercise 2: Is the first nested *for* loop in Prelab Exercise 1 processing the table by row or by column?

Is the second nested *for* loop processing the table by row or by column?

Is the third nested *for* loop processing the table by row or by column?

Lesson 12–1: Check Prelab Exercises

Name _____   Date _____

Section _____

Exercise 1: Run program Tables to see the output. Was your diagram correct? If not, do you understand what you did wrong?

Exercise 2: The first loop is processing by column; the second by row; the third by column.

Lesson 12-2: Two-Dimensional Arrays

Name _____ Date _____

Section _____

This lesson uses program TwoDTable.

```java
// Program TwoDTable manipulates a two-dimensional array
//  object

import java.io.*;
public class TwoDTable
{
  public TwoDTable(int rows, int cols)
  {
    table = new int[rows][cols];
  }

  public void  getTable(BufferedReader inFile)
    throws IOException
// Reads values from inFile and stores them in the table;
//  rowsUsed and colsUsed are in the first two lines of the file;
//  values follow by row, one value per line
  {
    /* TO BE FILLED IN: Exercise 1 */
  }

  public void  printTable()
// Writes values in the table on System.out
  {
    /* TO BE FILLED IN: Exercise 1 */
  }

  // Data fields
  int rowsUsed;
  int colsUsed;
  int[][] table;
}

import java.io.*;
public class UseTable
{
  public static void main(String[] args) throws IOException
  {
    TwoDTable  table;
    table = new TwoTable(10, 8);

    BufferedReader inFile = new BufferedReader(
      new FileReader("twod.dat"));

    table.getTable(inFile);
    table.printTable();
    inFile.close();
```

```
    }
}
```

Exercise 1: Read the documentation carefully and complete program `TwoDTable`. Show what is printed.

_____ _____ _____ _____ _____

_____ _____ _____ _____ _____

_____ _____ _____ _____ _____

_____ _____ _____ _____ _____

Exercise 2: Add a method that prints the largest value in `table`. Rerun the program.

Largest value is _____.

Exercise 3: Add a method that prints the smallest value in `table`. Rerun the program.

Smallest value is _____.

Exercise 4: Add a method that sums the values in a column of `table`. Pass the column you want to sum as a parameter. Call your function to print the sum of each column appropriately labeled.

Sum of Column 1 is _____.   Sum of Column 2 is _____.

Sum of Column 3 is _____.   Sum of Column 4 is _____.

Sum of Column 5 is _____.

Exercise 5: The specifications on the data have been changed. The data is to be entered by columns rather than by rows. In addition, the order of `rowsUsed` and `colsUsed` has been reversed; that is, `colsUsed` is the first value and `rowsUsed` is the second value. Rewrite function `GetTable` to input `table` using the new specifications. Run your program using `twodalt.dat`.

Smallest value is   _____.

Largest value is   _____.

Sum of Column 1 is _____.

Sum of Column 2 is _____.

Sum of Column 3 is _____.

Sum of Column 4 is _____.

Sum of Column 5 is _____.

Exercise 6: Rewrite your program assuming that the data is stored on the file as follows rather than one data value per line.

```
number of rows, number of columns
first row
second row
...
last row
```

For example, `twoD.dat` would look this way:

```
4 5
3 1 3 1 5
2 3 6 7 1
7 8 8 8 8
9 8 7 6 5
```

Recompile and rerun Exercise 4. (*Hint:* Use `indexOf` and `substring`.)

Lesson 12-3: Multidimensional Arrays

Name _____ Date _____

Section _____

Use shell `ThreeDTable` for Exercises 1 through 3.

```java
public class ThreeDTable
{
  public ThreeDTable(int first, int second, int third)
  {
    /* TO BE FILLED IN: Exercise 1 */
  }
  public void setValue(int first, int second, int third,
    char data)
  {
    /* TO BE FILLED IN: Exercise 2 */
  }
  public void print()
  {
    /* TO BE FILLED IN: Exercise 3 */
  }

  // Data fields
  char[][][] values;

}
```

Exercise 1: Fill in the body of the constructor that instantiates the array using the three parameters.

Exercise 2: Fill in the body of method `setValue` that stores a data value in the position indicated by the parameters.

Exercise 3: Fill in the body of method `print` that prints `values`.

Exercise 4: Write a driver that defines a three-dimensional table with dimensions 3, 2, and 4, stores an asterisk (*) in every position in the table, and prints the table.

Lesson 12-4: Debugging

Name _____ Date _____

Section _____

Exercise 1: Class `Mystery` reads data into a two-dimensional array. The data is input as described in Lesson 12-2, Exercise 6. The data file is shown below:

```
3 4
1 2 3 4
5 6 7 8
9 8 7 6
```

Unfortunately, program `UseMystery`, a driver for class `Mystery`, demonstrates errors. Can you find and fix it? Describe the error.

Exercise 2: Unless you found more than one error in Exercise 1, there are still problems lurking in class `Mystery`. Correct the error(s) and rerun the program. Describe the error(s).

Postlab Activities

Exercise 1: Two-dimensional arrays are good structures to represent boards in games. Create a class `Board`. The constructor takes a size as a parameter and instantiates a square array. Write a method `placeSymbol` that takes a symbol as a parameter and places that symbol in all of the cells of the board. Write another method `placeSymbols` that takes two symbols and places them in alternating patterns like a checkerboard. Write a third method that prints the checkerboard on the screen. Write a fourth method that takes a symbol and a row and column designation and places the symbol on the board at that row and column. If the row and column are not within the dimensions of the board, throw an exception.

Exercise 2: Write a test plan for class `Board` and implement it.

Exercise 3: Write a program that keeps track of stock prices for five stocks for one week. Choose any five stocks on the New York Stock Exchange. Use actual stock prices for one week as your data. Include the clippings from the paper with your program.

Your program should be interactive. Prompt the user to enter the names of the five stocks. Then prompt the user to enter a week's worth of prices for each stock. The program should print the table showing the stock values for a week, the average daily value of the stocks, and the average price for each stock for the week.

Exercise 4: Write a test plan for the class in Exercise 3 and implement it.

Recursion

- To be able to write a recursive value-returning method to solve a problem involving simple variables.

- To be able to write a recursive void method to solve a problem involving simple variables.

- To be able to write a recursive value-returning method to solve a problem involving structured objects.

- To be able to write a recursive void method to solve a problem involving structured objects.

Laboratory 13: Assignment Cover Sheet

Name _____ Date _____

Section _____

Fill in the following table showing which exercises have been assigned for each lesson and check what you are to submit: (1) lab sheets, (2) listings of output files, and/or (3) listings of code. Your instructor or teaching assistant (TA) can use the Completed column for grading purposes.

Activities	Assigned: Check or list exercise numbers	Submit (1) (2) (3)			Completed
Prelab					
Review					
Prelab Assignment					
Inlab					
Lesson 13-1: Check Prelab Exercises					
Lesson 13-2: Simple Variables					
Lesson 13-3: Structured Objects					
Lesson 13-4: Debugging					
Postlab					

Prelab Activities

Review

When a method invokes itself, the call is known as a *recursive* call. Recursion—the ability of a method to call itself—is an alternative control structure to repetition (looping). Rather than use a *while* statement, *do* statement, or *for* statement to execute a segment of code again, the program uses a selection statement (*if* or *switch* statement) to determine whether to repeat the code by calling the method again or to stop the process.

Each recursive solution has at least two cases: the *base case* and the *general case*. The base case is the one to which we have an answer; the general case expresses the solution in terms of a call to itself with a smaller version of the problem. Because the general case solves a smaller and smaller version of the original problem, eventually the program reaches the base case where an answer is known and the recursion stops.

Simple Variables

Associated with each recursive problem is some measure of the size of the problem. The size must get smaller with each recursive call. The first step in any recursive solution is to determine the *size factor*. If the problem involves a numerical value, the size factor might be the value itself. For example, a classic recursive problem is the factorial. The factorial of a number is defined as the product of all the numbers between itself and 0: $N! = N * (N-1)!$. The factorial of 0 is 1. The size factor is the number for which we are calculating the factorial. We have a base case, factorial(0) is 1, and we have a general case, factorial(N) is $N *$ factorial(N-1). An *if* statement can evaluate N to see if it is 0 (the base case) or greater than 0 (the general case). Because N is clearly getting smaller with each call, the base case is reached.

```
public long factorial(long n)
// Assumption:  n is not negative.
{
  if (n == 0)
    return 1;                     // Base case
  else
    return n * factorial(n-1);  // General case
}
```

What happens if n is a negative number? The method just keeps calling itself until the runtime support system runs out of memory. This situation is called *infinite recursion* and is equivalent to an infinite loop. If infinite recursion occurs, the program may crash with a message such as "RUN-TIME STACK OVERFLOW" or the program (and the screen) may just freeze.

Structured Variables

If we are working with structures rather than single values, the size is often the number of items in the structure. For example, if we want to count the number of items in a list, the base case is when the list is empty: There are no items in an empty list. In a nonempty list, the number of items is one plus the number of items in the rest of the list.

When using recursion with structures, it is the structure that is getting smaller, not the class in which the structure is a member. For example, in the case of counting the number of items in an array-based list, the recursion is on the array. The parameters of the recursion are the beginning point of the list in the array and the number of items.

Let's write a recursive method to print the items in an array-based list. The recursive method is implemented as a helper method that is called by the instance method in the class.

```java
public class List
{
  final int MAX_LENGTH = 20;
  int[] list;
  int  numItems;
  private void printList(int first, int last)
  // The items are printed on System.out recursively
  {
    if (first < last)
    {
      System.out.println(list[first]);
      printList(first+1, last);
    }
  }

  public void print()
  {
    printList(0, numItems);
  }
  // Methods to manipulate the list
  ...
}
```

When using recursion with structured variables, the base case can be a "do nothing" case as in the last example. The instance method print is called, which then calls the helper method printList with 0 and numItems as the arguments. The 0 replaces first and numItems replaces last. If first is less than last, list[first] is printed and printList is called with first plus one. Eventually first becomes equal to last (numItems), and all the items in the list have been printed.

Recursion is a very powerful and elegant tool. However, not all problems can easily be solved recursively, and not all problems that have an obvious recursive solution should be solved recursively. But there are many problems for which a recursive solution is preferable. If the problem statement logically falls into two cases, a base case and a general case, you should consider a recursive solution.

Laboratory 13: Prelab Assignment

Name _____ Date _____

Section _____

Exercise 1: Fill in the following chart showing the value of the variable n at the beginning of each execution of method `factorial`, starting with the nonrecursive call `factorial(5)`. Fill in the third column with the method value returned at the completion of the execution of that call.

Call	n	Method Value Returned
Nonrecursive Call		
1st Recursive Call		
2nd Recursive Call		
3rd Recursive Call		
4th Recursive Call		
5th Recursive Call		

Exercise 2: Fill in the chart showing the value of the variables `first` and `last` at the beginning of each execution of method `printList`. Here is the array being printed. The length is 15 and `numItems` is 5.

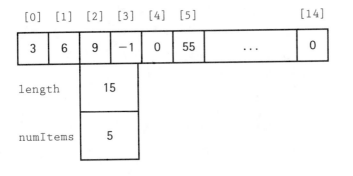

[0]	[1]	[2]	[3]	[4]	[5]		[14]
3	6	9	−1	0	55	...	0

length   15

numItems   5

Call	first	last	What is printed
Nonrecursive Call			
1st Recursive Call			
2nd Recursive Call			
3rd Recursive Call			
4th Recursive Call			
5th Recursive Call			
6th Recursive Call			

Lesson 13-1: Check Prelab Exercises

Name _____ Date _____

Section _____

Exercise 1:

Call	n	Method Value Returned
Nonrecursive Call	5	120
1st Recursive Call	4	24
2nd Recursive Call	3	6
3rd Recursive Call	2	2
4th Recursive Call	1	1
5th Recursive Call	0	1

Exercise 2:

Call	first	last	What is printed
Nonrecursive Call	0	5	3
1st Recursive Call	1	5	6
2nd Recursive Call	2	5	9
3rd Recursive Call	3	5	−1
4th Recursive Call	4	5	0
5th Recursive Call	5	5	
6th Recursive Call			

Lesson 13-2: Simple Variables

Name _____ Date _____

Section _____

Exercise 1: Java does not have an exponential operator. Write the recursive value-returning method power that takes two parameters (number and exponent) and returns number multiplied by itself exponent times. That is, power returns the result of number^{exponent}. Run a driver program that calls power(7, 3) and prints the result.

What is printed?

Exercise 2: The Fibonacci numbers are defined as the following sequence:

1 1 2 3 5 8 13 21 34 55 ...

Notice that except for the first two numbers, each number is the sum of the two preceding numbers. Write a recursive value-returning method, fib, which returns the Nth Fibonacci number where N is a parameter. Test your program with fib(5), fib(10), and fib(20).

Show your output.

Exercise 3: Write an iterative version of method fib and test it with the same values.

Exercise 4: You have just demonstrated that the Fibonacci numbers can be generated recursively and iteratively. If you need them in a program, which version do you use? Justify your answer.

Lesson 13-3: Structured Objects

Name _____ Date _____

Section _____

Exercise 1: Write a recursive void method that prints out the values in a list in reverse order.

Exercise 2: Did you use one or two parameters to your print method? If you used two, could you have gotten by with only using one?

Exercise 3: Write a recursive `int` method that returns the position of a given value in a list. If the value is not in the list, return −1. For example, given the following list and a value of 9, the method would return 2.

```
    [0]  [1]  [2]  [3]  [4]  [5]              [14]
   ┌────┬────┬────┬────┬────┬────┬─────────┬────┐
   │ 3  │ 6  │ 9  │ −1 │ 0  │ 55 │   ...   │ 0  │
   └────┴────┴────┴────┴────┴────┴─────────┴────┘

   length      ┌─────┐
               │ 15  │
               ├─────┤
   numItems    │  5  │
               └─────┘
```

Exercise 4: Write a test driver for your method in Exercise 3. Use the list shown above. Run your driver asking for the positions of 3, 6, −1, and 55. Record the results.

Lesson 13–4: Debugging

Name _____ Date _____

Section _____

Exercise 1: In order to practice writing recursive processes, you decide to write a recursive method to sum the values in a file. Program SumTest is the result, but it isn't working. Debug it.

List the errors found and what you did to correct them. (*Hint:* There are two.)

Postlab Activities

Exercise 1: How many possible bridge hands are there? This question is a specific case of the general question: How many combinations of X items can you make out of Y items? In the case of the bridge hand, X is 13 and Y is 52. The solution is given by the following formula:

Combinations(Y, X) =

Y	if $X = 1$
1	if $X = Y$
(Combinations(Y-1, X-1) + Combinations(Y-1, X))	if $Y > X > 1$

Write a recursive method that calculates the number of combinations of X items that can be made from Y items. Write a driver and answer the original questions.

Exercise 2: Write and implement a test plan for Exercise 1, Lesson 13-3. Is this a good use of recursion? Justify your answer.

Exercise 3: Write a recursive `boolean` method, `isThere`, that searches a sorted, array-based list for a value and returns `true` if the value is there and `false` otherwise.

Exercise 4: Write and implement a test plan for Exercise 3 above. Is Exercise 3 a good use of recursion? Justify your answer.

Exercise 5: In Laboratory 11, we described the binary search algorithm. This algorithm is an inherently recursive algorithm, though it is often implemented iteratively. Take the code for class `SList` as developed in Lesson 11-3, Exercises 1 through 5. Write recursive method `binSrch` as a helper method in `SList`. Change the code of each member method that requires a search, to use `binSrch`. Test your class using the driver written for Exercise 6 in Lesson 11-3.

Applets

- To be able to convert an application to an applet.

- To be able to write an applet to perform a simple task.

- To be able to write an HTML document that contains an applet.

- To be able to create and run an applet on the Web.

Laboratory 14: Assignment Cover Sheet

Name _____ Date _____

Section _____

Fill in the following table showing which exercises have been assigned for each lesson and check what you are to submit: (1) lab sheets, (2) listings of output files, and/or (3) listings of code. Your instructor or teaching assistant (TA) can use the Completed column for grading purposes.

Activities	Assigned: Check or list exercise numbers	Submit (1)	(2)	(3)	Completed
Prelab					
Review					
Prelab Assignment					
Inlab					
Lesson 14-1: Check Prelab Exercises					
Lesson 14-2: Convert an Application to an Applet					
Lesson 14-3: Write an Applet					
Lesson 14-4: Create a Web Page					
Lesson 14-5: Run an Applet on the Web					
Postlab					

Prelab Activities

Review

In Laboratory 2, we defined a Java application as a class with a method named main. Java supports a second type of program called an *applet*, which does not run as a stand-alone program, but is executed within a Web browser.

Differences between Applications and Applets

Because an applet runs under a Web browser, it doesn't have a main method. It is much more like a windowing component than a stand-alone application. An applet responds when told to do so by the browser or viewer; it is not in control of its own execution.

An applet is embedded within an HTML document and thus not invoked in the same fashion as an application. HTML is the language used to create Web pages. We later describe enough HTML to allow you to write a Web page that includes an applet.

Because applets are distributed over the Web, they are subjected to more security constraints than an application. For example, they cannot change files on the viewer's computer.

Structure of an Applet

Let's go through the structure of an applet by looking at an example. We intersperse comments within the program, pointing out similarities and differences between applications and applets.

The following applet asks the user to enter the size of a list to be sorted, generates the list, sorts the list, and prints the sorted values. Let's first examine the packages that must be imported.

```
// Applet Sorts sorts an array of random values.

import java.util.*;        // Supplies random number generator
import java.awt.*;         // Supplies layout manager
import java.awt.event.*;   // Supplies event classes
import java.applet.Applet; // Supplies class Applet
```

The random number generator is used to generate the list of random values. Packages awt and awt.event provide the layout manager, abstract class ActionListener, labels, buttons, and text fields.

All applets are explicitly derived from class Applet[1], just as all applications are implicitly derived from class Object. Thus, the class heading must extend class Applet. We said that an applet is like a windowing component, so it is no surprise that the applet must implement ActionListener. Here is the class heading.

```
public class Sorts extends Applet implements ActionListener
```

All applets must have this heading.

---

[1] There is a JApplet class which is part of the swing package. However many older browsers are not set up to accept Swing applets, and those that are can still run AWT applets.

What actions take place when the user enters a number and presses the enter button? The number must be input and converted to numeric form, an array of that size must be generated and initialized with random values, the array must be sorted, and the values printed. We can write the `actionPerformed` method first and then write the helper methods that carry out these tasks.

```java
public void actionPerformed(ActionEvent event)
// Event handler method
{
  size = Short.parseShort(inputField.getText());
  values = new int[size];    // Generate the array
  initValues(size);          // Fill the array
  selectionSort();           // Sort the array
  printValues();             // Print the array
  inputField.setText("");    // Reset input field
}
```

`initValues` takes the number of values to be generated as a parameter and randomly generates this many values. Here is the code for method `initValues`. Notice that the values being generated are scaled to between zero and the number of values minus one.

```java
void initValues(int size)
// Initializes the values array with random
//   integers from 0 to size - 1
{
  Random rand = new Random();
  for (int index = 0; index < size; index++)
    values[index] = Math.abs(rand.nextInt()) % size;
}
```

There are many different sorting algorithms. One of the simplest is called *selection sort*. You find the smallest value in the array and swap it with the value in the first array position. Next you find the smallest value in the rest of the array and swap it with the value in the second position. Then you find the smallest value in the array beginning at the third position and swap it with the value in the third position. The process continues until the array is completely sorted.

To code this algorithm we use two helper methods: `minIndex`, which returns the index of the minimum value in the array bounded by its parameters (the part of the array not yet sorted) and `swap`, which swaps the contents of two places.

```java
int minIndex(int startIndex, int endIndex)
// Post: Returns the index of the smallest value in
//        values[startIndex]..values[endIndex]
{
  int indexOfMin = startIndex;
  for (int index = startIndex + 1; index <= endIndex;
       index++)
    if (values[index] < values[indexOfMin])
      indexOfMin = index;
  return indexOfMin;
}
```

```
public void swap(int index1, int index2)
// Swaps the integers at locations index1 and index2
//  of array values
// Precondition: index1 and index2 are less than size
{
  int temp = values[index1];
  values[index1] = values[index2];
  values[index2] = temp;
}

void selectionSort()
// Post: The elements in the array values are sorted
{
  int endIndex = size - 1;
  for (int current = 0; current < endIndex; current++)
    swap(current, minIndex(current, endIndex));
}
```

The only task left is to print the values in the array. Let's print them ten to a line to keep the output from being so long.

```
void printValues()
// Prints all the values
{
  int value;
  for (int index = 0; index < size; index++)
  {
    value = values[index];
    if (((index + 1) % 10) == 0)
      System.out.println(value);
    else
      System.out.print(value + " ");
  }
  System.out.println();
}
```

Since all the processing is done within the `actionPerformed` method, all that is left is to declare the variables and set up the input window. What variables do we need in addition to `size` and `values`? We need a text field, a label, and a button. The label and the button can be declared within method `init`, but `size`, `values`, and the text field must be declared where they are visible to method `actionPerformed` and the helper methods.

```
// Declaring fields

private TextField inputField;
private int[] values; // Values to be sorted
private int size;     // Number of values to sort
```

We have to instantiate the text field, declare and instantiate a label, and declare, instantiate, and register a listener with a button. The window components are the same that you used in Laboratory 8, except that the "J" is removed.

```
public void init()
{
  Button button;
  Label label;
  label = new Label("Enter list size; press Enter.");
  button = new Button("Enter");
  button.addActionListener(this);

  inputField = new TextField("Value here");

  // Add window components; no pane is needed
  add(inputField);
  add(button);
  add(label);
  setLayout(new GridLayout(0,1));
  }
}
```

See how much easier it is to set up a window in an applet? You don't need to declare a frame or add elements to a frame (or pane). In most applets, the applet itself is the listener, so you don't have to declare a separate listener class. You just use `this` as the argument for `addActionListener`.

HTML

The Hypertext Markup Language (HTML) is the language used to generate Web pages. The primary elements of the language are tags that we insert into the document to indicate how the information should be displayed. Tags are enclosed in angled brackets, and many of the tags come in pairs with the closing tag beginning with a slash. The following table shows some of the more useful tags. Although we use uppercase for the tags, HTML is not case sensitive.

Tags	Meaning
<HTML> ... </HTML>	Beginning and end of an HTML document
<TITLE> ... </TITLE>	Enclose the title of the document
<P> ... </P>	Enclose a paragraph
<HR>	Writes a horizontal rule
<B> ... </B>	Enclosed text is boldface
<PRE> ... </PRE>	Display text exactly as keyed
<APPLET> ... </APPLET>	Specifies an applet to be run

The opening <APPLET> tag is more complex than the others because it must include the name of the applet to run and the size of the window on the screen. To run applet `Sorts`, you would use the following code:

```
<APPLET code = "Sorts.class" width = 250 height = 150></APPLET>
```

The phrase code = "`Sorts.class`" specifies which applet to run. Most compilers store the Bytecode file under the name of the class with a `.class` extension. The system you are using may require you to explicitly name the Bytecode file. Just remember that it needs a `.class` extension.

Laboratory 14: Prelab Assignment

Name _____ Date _____

Section _____

Exercise 1: What would the window in the applet look like if `GridLayout` was called with (0, 3)? Draw a picture.

Exercise 2: What would happen if the values generated by the random number generator were not scaled?

Exercise 3: What statement would scale the random numbers generated to between -99 and 99?

Lesson 14-1: Check Prelab Exercises

Name _____ Date _____

Section _____

Exercise 1: Run the applet in file Sorts2 to check your answer. Were you correct? If not, do you understand what you did wrong?

Exercise 2: Run the applet in file Sorts3 to check your answer. Were you correct? If not, do you understand what you did wrong?

Exercise 3: The applet in file Sorts4 is set to generate the values within the proper range. Run the applet and examine the statement that does this scaling. Were you correct? If not, do you understand what you did wrong?

Lesson 14-2: Convert an Application to an Applet

Name _____ Date _____

Section _____

Exercises 1-5 convert application OddEven into an applet. Run application OddEven to be sure you understand what it does.

```java
import java.io.*;

public class OddEven
// This application inputs a three-digit number and
//  prints whether each digit is odd or even.
{
  public static void main(String[] args) throws IOException
  {
    BufferedReader inData;                    // Input stream
    int number;

    inData =
      new BufferedReader(new InputStreamReader(System.in));
    System.out.println("Enter a three digit number. ");
    number = Integer.parseInt(inData.readLine());
    if ((number / 2) * 2 == number)
      System.out.println("Unit's position is even.");
    else
      System.out.println("Unit's position is odd.");
    if ((((number / 10) / 2) * 2) == (number / 10))
      System.out.println("Ten's position is even.");
    else
      System.out.println("Ten's position is odd.");
    if ((((number / 100) / 2) * 2) == (number / 100))
      System.out.println("Hundred's position is even.");
    else
      System.out.println("Hundred's position is odd.");
  }
}
```

Exercise 1: Write the class heading and shell for applet OddEven.

Exercise 2: Write the actionPerformed method for the applet OddEven.

Exercise 3: Write the declarations for the variables needed in applet `OddEven`.

Exercise 4: Write method `init` for applet `OddEven`.

Exercise 5: Put Exercises 1-4 together and compile and run applet `OddEven`.

Exercise 6: Applet `OddEven` has a functionality that application `OddEven` does not have. What is it and how could you give this functionality to the application?

Lesson 14-3: Write an Applet

Name _____ Date _____

Section _____

Exercise 1: Write, compile, and test an applet that prompts for and reads an integer number and prints whether the number of digits in the number is odd or even. List your test cases.

Exercise 2: Write, compile, and test an applet that prompts for and reads a string and prints the string in reverse order.

Exercise 3: Write, compile, and test an applet that prompts for a month, day, and year, and prints the date in American form (month, day, and year) and English form (day, month, and year). Be sure to label your output properly.

Lesson 14–4: Create a Web Page

Name _____ Date _____

Section _____

Exercise 1: Use HTML to write a title containing your name to be used on a Web page.

Exercise 2: Write two horizontal bars under the title.

Exercise 3: Write a paragraph welcoming viewers to your Web page.

Exercise 4: Write an applet that asks a viewer for his or her name and thanks them by name for visiting your Web page.

Exercise 5: Write the statements that cause the applet to be executed when a browser copies your Web page.

Exercise 6: Tie Exercises 1-5 together with the tags that make the results a complete HTML document.

Lesson 14-5: Run an Applet on the Web

Name _____ Date _____

Section _____

This Lesson requires that you have the ability to put a page up on the Web. If your instructor does not provide you with this access, contact the Jones and Bartlett Web site at http://computerscience.jbpub.com/ppsJava/ and click on the Student Resources section of the site. Check with your instructor about the available software to allow you to transport files.

Exercise 1: Ship your HTML document to a Web site.

Exercise 2: Ship the Bytecode version of your applet to the Web site.

Exercise 3: Visit your Web page, enter your name, and print the screen. Have a friend visit your Web page and print the screen.

Postlab Activities

Exercise 1: Write an applet that prompts for and reads a `byte` value. Sum the numbers from 0 through the number that was entered and print this value. Prompt the user to continue entering values until the sum turns negative (is garbage). What is the largest value whose sum can be correctly stored in a variable of type `byte`?

Exercise 2: Rewrite the applet in Exercise 1 so that the input values are of type `int`. What is the largest value whose sum can be correctly stored in a variable of type `int`?

Exercise 3: Create a Web site for the Kitty Kat Naming Company. The purpose of this company is to take owner's names and generate possible names for the viewer's cat. Prompt for and read the viewer's name and generate possible names. You may use any algorithm that occurs to you. Transfer your files and run this application on the Web.

Appendix A

Java Reserved Words

abstract	do	if	package	synchronized
boolean	double	implements	private	this
break	else	import	protected	throw
byte	extends	instanceof	public	throws
case	false	int	return	transient
catch	final	interface	short	true
char	finally	long	static	try
class	float	native	strictfp	void
const	for	new	super	volatile
continue	goto	null	switch	while
default				

Appendix B

Operator Precedence

Precedence (highest to lowest)

Operator	Assoc.*	Operand Types(s)	Operation Performed
.	LR	object, member	object member access
[]	LR	array, int	array element access
(args)	LR	method, arglist	method invocation
++, --	LR	variable	post-increment, decrement
++, --	RL	variable	pre-increment, decrement
+, -	RL	number	unary plus, unary minus
~	RL	integer	bitwise complement
!	RL	boolean	boolean NOT
new	RL	class, arglist	object creation
(type)	RL	type, any	cast (type conversion)
*, /, %	LR	number, number	multiplication, division, remainder
+, -	LR	number, number	addition, subtraction
+	LR	string, any	string concatenation
<<	LR	integer, integer	left shift
>>	LR	integer, integer	right shift with sign extension
>>>	LR	integer, integer	right shift with zero extension
<, <=	LR	number, number	less than, less than or equal
>, >=	LR	number, number	greater than, greater than or equal
instanceof	LR	reference, type	type comparison
==	LR	primitive, primitive	equal (have identical values)
!=	LR	primitive, primitive	not equal (have different values)
==	LR	reference, reference	equal (refer to the same object)
!=	LR	reference, reference	not equal (refer to different objects)
&	LR	integer, integer	bitwise AND
&	LR	boolean, boolean	boolean AND
^	LR	integer, integer	bitwise XOR
^	LR	boolean, boolean	boolean XOR

Precedence (highest to lowest) (continued)

Operator	Assoc.*	Operand Types(s)	Operation Performed
|	LR	integer, integer	bitwise OR
|	LR	boolean, boolean	boolean OR
&&	LR	boolean, boolean	conditional AND (short circuit evaluation)
||	LR	boolean, boolean	conditional OR (short circuit evaluation)
? :	RL	boolean, any, any	conditional (ternary) operator
=	RL	variable, any	assignment
*=, /=, %=, +=, -=, <<=, >>=, >>>=, &=, ^=, |=	RL	variable, any	assignment with operation

*LR means left to right associativity; RL means right to left associativity.

Appendix C

Primitive Data Types

Type	Value Stored	Default Value	Size	Range of Values
char	Unicode character	Character code 0	16 bits	0 to 65535
byte	Integer value	0	8 bits	−128 to 127
short	Integer value	0	16 bits	−32768 to 32767
int	Integer value	0	32 bits	−2147483648 to 2147483647
long	Integer value	0	64 bits	−9223372036854775808 to 9223372036854775807
float	Real value	0.0	32 bits	±1.4E-45 to ±3.4028235E+38
double	Real value	0.0	64 bits	±4.9E-324 to ±1.7976931348623157E+308
boolean	true or false	false	1 bit	NA

Appendix D

ASCII Subset of Unicode

The following charts show the ordering of characters in two widely used character sets: ASCII (American Standard Code for Information Interchange) and EBCDIC (Extended Binary Coded Decimal Interchange Code). The internal representation for each character is shown in decimal. For example, the letter *A* is represented internally as the integer 65 in ASCII and as 193 in EBCDIC. The space (blank) character is denoted by a "□".

Left Digit(s) \ Right Digit	0	1	2	3	4	5	6	7	8	9
				ASCII						
0	NUL	SOH	STX	ETX	EOT	ENQ	ACK	BEL	BS	HT
1	LF	VT	FF	CR	SO	SI	DLE	DC1	DC2	DC3
2	DC4	NAK	SYN	ETB	CAN	EM	SUB	ESC	FS	GS
3	RS	US	□	!	"	#	$	%	&	'
4	(	)	*	+	,	−	.	/	0	1
5	2	3	4	5	6	7	8	9	:	;
6	<	=	>	?	@	A	B	C	D	E
7	F	G	H	I	J	K	L	M	N	O
8	P	Q	R	S	T	U	V	W	X	Y
9	Z	[	\	]	^	_	`	a	b	c
10	d	e	f	g	h	i	j	k	l	m
11	n	o	p	q	r	s	t	u	v	w
12	x	y	z	{			}	~	DEL		

Codes 00–31 and 127 are the following nonprintable control characters:

NUL	Null character	VT	Vertical tab	SYN	Synchronous idle
SOH	Start of header	FF	Form feed	ETB	End of transmitted block
STX	Start of text	CR	Carriage return	CAN	Cancel
ETX	End of text	SO	Shift out	EM	End of medium
EOT	End of transmission	SI	Shift in	SUB	Substitute
ENQ	Enquiry	DLE	Data link escape	ESC	Escape
ACK	Acknowledge	DC1	Device control one	FS	File separator
BEL	Bell character (beep)	DC2	Device control two	GS	Group separator
BS	Back space	DC3	Device control three	RS	Record separator
HT	Horizontal tab	DC4	Device control four	US	Unit separator
LF	Line feed	NAK	Negative acknowledge	DEL	Delete

abstract   a modifier of a class or field that indicates that it is incomplete and must be fully defined in a derived class

abstract data type (ADT)   a class of data objects with a defined set of properties and a set of operations that process the data objects while maintaining the properties

abstract step   an algorithmic step for which some implementation details remain unspecified

abstraction   a model of a complex system that includes only the details essential to the perspective of the viewer of the system; the separation of the logical properties of data or actions from their implementation details; the separation of the logical properties of an object from its implementation

abstraction (in OOD)   the essential characteristics of an object from the viewpoint of the user

aggregate operation   an operation on a data structure as a whole, as opposed to an operation on an individual component of the data structure

algorithm   a logical sequence of discrete steps that describes a complete solution to a given problem computable in a finite amount of time; instructions for solving a problem or subproblem in a finite amount of time using a finite amount of data; a verbal or written description of a logical sequence of actions

allocate   to assign memory space at run time for use by an object

ALU   see *arithmetic/logic unit*

anonymous class   a class that does not have an identifier (a name) associated with it

argument   a variable, constant, or expression listed in the call to a method

arithmetic/logic unit (ALU)   the component of the central processing unit that performs arithmetic and logical operations

array   a collection of components, all of the same type, ordered on *n* dimensions (*n* >= 1); each component is accessed by *n* indices, each of which represents the component's position within that dimension

assembler   a program that translates an assembly language program into machine code

assembly language   a low-level programming language in which a mnemonic represents each of the machine language instructions for a particular computer

assertion   a logical proposition that is either true or false

assignment expression   a Java expression with (1) a value and (2) the side effect of storing the expression value into a memory location

assignment statement   a statement that stores the value of an expression into a variable

asynchronous   not occurring at the same moment in time as some specific operation of the computer; in other words, not synchronized with the program's actions

atomic data type   a data type that allows only a single value to be associated with an identifier of that type

auxiliary storage device   a device that stores data in encoded form outside the computer's memory

binary operator   an operator that has two operands

base address   the memory address of the first element of an array

base case   the case for which the solution can be stated nonrecursively

base class   the class being inherited from

big-O notation   a notation that expresses computing time (complexity) as the term in a function that increases most rapidly relative to the size of a problem

binary   expressed in terms of combinations of the numbers 1 and 0 only

binary search   a search algorithm for sorted lists that involves dividing the list in half and determining, by value comparison, whether the item would be in the upper or lower half; the process is performed repeatedly until either the item is found or it is determined that the item is not on the list

bit   short for binary digit; a single 1 or 0

block   a group of zero or more statements enclosed in braces

body   the statement(s) to be repeated within the loop; the executable statement(s) within a function

boolean   a data type consisting of only two values: true and false

boolean expression   an assertion that is evaluated as either true or false, the only values of the boolean data type

boolean operators   operators applied to values of the type boolean; in Java these are the special symbols &&, ||, and !

booting the system   the process of starting up a computer by loading the operating system into its main memory

branch   a code segment that is not always executed; for example, a switch statement has as many branches as there are case labels

branching control structure   see *selection control structure*

brainstorming (in OOD)   the beginning phase of an object-oriented design in which possible classes of objects in the problem are identified

button   a component that fires an event (called a *button event*) when the user clicks on it with the mouse

byte   eight bits

Bytecode   a standard machine language into which Java source code is compiled

CRC Cards   index cards on which a class name is written along with its super and subclasses and a listing of the class's responsibilities and collaborators; Class, *R*esponsibility, *C*ollaboration

call   the point at which the computer begins following the instructions in a subprogram is referred to as the subprogram call

cancellation error   a form of representational error that occurs when numbers of widely differing magnitudes are added or subtracted

catch   the processing of a thrown exception by a section of code called an exception handler

central processing unit (CPU)   the part of the computer that executes the instructions (program) stored in memory; consists of the arithmetic/logic unit and the control unit

char   data type whose values consist of one alphanumeric character (letter, digit, or special symbol)

character set   a standard set of alphanumeric characters with a given collating sequence and binary representation

class (general sense)   a description of the behavior of a group of objects with similar properties and behaviors

class (Java construct)   a pattern for an object

class data   data that is associated with a class and accessible by all objects of that class

class method   a method that is associated with a class but not with a specific object; it is called by writing the name of the class followed by a period and then the name of the method and its parameter list

client   software that declares and manipulates objects of a particular class

code   data type specifications and instructions for a computer that are written in a programming language

code walk-through   a verification process for a program in which each statement is examined to check that it faithfully implements the corresponding algorithmic step

coding   translating an algorithm into a programming language; the process of assigning bit patterns to pieces of information

collating sequence   the ordering of the elements of a set or series, such as the characters (values) in a character set

compiler   a program that translates a high-level language (such as C++, Pascal, or Java) into machine code

compiler listing   a copy of a program into which have been inserted messages from the compiler (indicating errors in the program that prevent its translation into machine language if appropriate)

complexity   a measure of the effort expended by the computer in performing a computation, relative to the size of the computation

composite data type   a data type that allows a collection of values to be associated with an object of that type

composition (containment)   a mechanism by which an internal data member of one class is defined to be an object of another class type

computer (electronic)   a programmable device that can store, retrieve, and process data

computer program   data type specifications and instructions for carrying out operations that are used by a computer to solve a problem

computer programming   the process of specifying the data types and the operations for a computer to apply to data in order to solve a problem

concrete step   a step for which the implementation details are fully specified

conditional test   the point at which the boolean expression is evaluated and the decision is made to either begin a new iteration or skip to the first statement following the loop

constant   an item in a program whose value is fixed at compile time and cannot be changed during execution

constant time   an algorithm whose big-O work expression is a constant

constructor   an operation that creates a new instance of a class; a method that has the same name as the class type containing it, which is called whenever an object of that type is instantiated

container class   a class into which you can add other elements

control abstraction   the separation of the logical properties of a control structure from its implementation

control structure   a statement used to alter the normally sequential flow of control

control unit   the component of the central processing unit that controls the action of other components so that instructions (the program) are executed in sequence

conversion function   a function that converts a value of one type to another type so that it can be assigned to a variable of the second type; also called transfer function or type cast

copy constructor   an operation that creates a new instance of a class by copying an existing instance, possibly altering some or all of its state in the process

count-controlled loop   a loop that executes a predetermined number of times

counter   a variable whose value is incremented to keep track of the number of times a process or event occurs

CPU   see *central processing unit*

crash   the cessation of a computer's operations as a result of the failure of one of its components; cessation of program execution due to an error

data   information that has been put into a form a computer can use

data abstraction   the separation of a data type's logical properties from its implementation

data encapsulation   the separation of the representation of data from the applications that use the data at a logical level; a programming language feature that enforces information hiding

data representation   the concrete form of data used to represent the abstract values of an abstract data type

data structure   a collection of data elements whose organization is characterized by accessing operations that are used to store and retrieve the individual data elements; the implementation of the composite data members in an abstract data type; the implementation of a composite data field in an abstract data type

data type   the general form of a class of data items; a formal description of the set of values (called the domain) and the basic set of operations that can be applied to it

data validation   a test added to a program or a function that checks for errors in the data

debugging   the process by which errors are removed from a program so that it does exactly what it is supposed to do

deallocate   to return the storage space for an object to the pool of free memory so that it can be reallocated to new objects

decision   see *selection control structure*

declaration   a statement that associates an identifier with a field, a method, a class, or a package so that the programmer can refer to that item by name

deep copy   an operation that not only copies one class object to another but also makes copies of any pointed-to data

demotion (narrowing)   the conversion of a value from a "higher" type to a "lower" type according to a programming language's precedence of data types; demotion may cause loss of information

derived class   a class that is created as an extension of another class in the hierarchy

desk checking   tracing an execution of a design or program on paper

development environment   a single package containing all of the software required for developing a program

dialog   a style of user interface in which the user enters data and then performs a separate action (such as clicking a button) when the entered values are ready to be processed by the program

direct execution   the process by which a computer performs the actions specified in a machine language program

documentation   the written text and comments that make a program easier for others to understand, use, and modify

down   a descriptive term applied to a computer when it is not in a usable condition

driver   a simple dummy main program that is used to call a method being tested; a main method in an object-oriented program

dynamic allocation   allocation of memory space for a variable at run time (as opposed to static allocation at compile time)

dynamic binding   determining at run time which form of a polymorphic method to call; the run-time determination of which implementation of an operation is appropriate

dynamic memory management   the allocation and deallocation of storage space as needed while an application is executing

echo printing   printing the data values input to a program to verify that they are correct

editor   an interactive program used to create and modify source programs or data

encapsulation (in OOD)   the bundling of data and actions in such a way that the logical properties of the data and actions are separated from the implementation details; the practice of hiding a module implementation in a separate block with a formally specified interface; designing a class so that its implementation is protected from the actions of external code except through the formal interface

evaluate   to compute a new value by performing a specified set of operations on given values

event   an action, such as a mouse click, that takes place asynchronously with respect to the execution of the program

event counter   a variable that is incremented each time a particular event occurs within a loop control structure

event handler   a method that is part of an event listener and is invoked when the listener receives a corresponding event

event handling   the process of responding to events that can occur at any time during execution of the program

event listener   an object that is waiting for one or more events to occur

event loop   The repetitive calling of an event handler to respond to a series of events until some condition causes the application to exit the cycle

event-controlled loop   a loop control structure that terminates when something happens inside the loop body to signal that the loop should be exited

exception   an unusual situation that is detected while a program is running; throwing an exception halts the normal execution of the method

exception handler   a section of a program that is executed when an exception occurs; in Java, an exception handler appears within a catch clause of a *try-catch-finally* control structure

executing   the action of a computer performing as instructed by a given program

execution trace   going through the program with actual values and recording the state of the variables

expression   an arrangement of identifiers, literals, and operators that can be evaluated to compute a value of a given type

expression statement   a statement formed by appending a semicolon to an expression

external file   a file that is used to communicate with people or programs and is stored externally to the program

external representation   the printable (character) form of a data value

fetch-execute cycle   the sequence of steps performed by the central processing unit for each machine language instruction

field   a component in which the user can type a value; the user must first place the cursor in the field by clicking inside the field; a named place in memory that holds a data value or a reference to an object

file a named area in secondary storage that is used to hold a collection of data; the collection of data itself

filtering (in OOD) the phase in an object-oriented design in which the proposed classes of objects from the brainstorming phase are refined and overlooked ones are added

finite state machine an idealized model of a simple computer consisting of a set of states, the rules that specify when states are changed, and a set of actions that are performed when changing states

firing an event an event source generates an event

flag a Boolean variable that is set in one part of the program and tested in another to control the logical flow of a program

flat implementation the hierarchical structure of a solution written as one long sequence of steps; also called inline implementation

floating point number the value stored in a type `float` or `double` variable, so called because part of the memory location holds the exponent and the balance of the location, the mantissa, with the decimal point floating as necessary among the significant digits

flow of control the order of execution of the statements in a program

formatting the planned positioning of statements or declarations and blanks on a line of a program; the arranging of program output so that it is neatly spaced and aligned

forward when a method calls another method that throws an exception, it may pass the exception to its own caller rather than catch the exception

free pool (heap) an area of memory, managed by the JVM, which is used to provide storage space for objects

functional decomposition a technique for developing software in which the problem is divided into more easily handled subproblems, the solutions of which create a solution to the overall problem

garbage the set of currently unreachable objects

garbage collection the process of finding all unreachable objects and destroying them by deallocating their storage space

general (recursive) case the case for which the solution is expressed in terms of a smaller version of itself

hardware the physical components of a computer

heuristics assorted problem-solving strategies

hide to provide a field in a derived class that has the same name as a field in its superclass; to provide a class method that has the same form of heading as a class method in its superclass; the field or class method is said to hide the corresponding component of the superclass

hierarchy (in OOD) structuring of abstractions in which a descendant object inherits the characteristics of its ancestors

high-level programming language any programming language in which a single statement translates into one or more machine language instructions

homogeneous a descriptive term applied to structures in which all components are of the same data type (such as an array)

identifier a name associated with a package, class, method, or field and used to refer to them

immutable an object whose state cannot be changed once it is created

implementation phase the second set of steps in programming a computer: translating (coding) the algorithm into a programming language; testing the resulting program by running it on a computer, checking for accuracy, and making any necessary corrections; using the program

implementing coding and testing an algorithm

implementing a test plan   running the program with the test cases listed in the test plan

implicit matching   see *positional matching*

in place   describes a kind of sorting algorithm in which the components in an array are sorted without the use of a second array

index   a value that selects a component of an array

infinite loop   a loop whose termination condition is never reached and which therefore is never exited without intervention from outside of the program

infinite recursion   the situation in which a subprogram calls itself over and over continuously

information   any knowledge that can be communicated

information hiding   the practice of hiding the details of a class with the goal of controlling access to them; the programming technique of hiding the details of data or actions from other parts of the program

inheritance   a design technique used with a hierarchy of classes by which each descendant class acquires the properties (data and operations) of its ancestor class; a mechanism that enables us to define a new class by adapting the definition of an existing class; a mechanism by which one class acquires the properties—the data fields and methods—of another class

inline implementation   see *flat implementation*

input   the process of placing values from an outside data set into variables in a program; the data may come from either an input device (keyboard) or an auxiliary storage device (disk or tape)

input prompts   messages printed by an interactive program, explaining what data is to be entered

input transformation   an operation that takes input values and converts them to the abstract data type representation

input/output (i/o) devices   the parts of a computer that accept data to be processed (input) and present the results of that processing (output)

inspection   a verification method in which one member of a team reads the program or design line by line and the others point out errors

instance data   data that is associated with a specific object

instance method   a method that is associated with an object of a given class; it is called by writing the name of the object followed by a period and then the name of the method and its parameter list

instantiate   to create an object based on the description supplied by a class

instantiation   creating an object, an instance of a class

integer number   a positive or negative whole number made up of a sign and digits (when the sign is omitted, a positive sign is assumed)

interactive system   a system that allows direct communication between the user and the computer

interface   a connecting link (such as a keyboard) at a shared boundary that allows independent systems (such as the user and the computer) to meet and act on or communicate with each other; the formal definition of the behavior of a subprogram and the mechanism for communicating with it; a Java construct that specifies method headings and constants to be included in any class that implements it

interpretation   the translation, while a program is running, of non-machine-language instructions (such as Bytecode) into executable operations

interpreter   a program that inputs a program in a high-level language and directs the computer to perform the actions specified in each statement; unlike a compiler, an interpreter does not produce a machine language version of the entire program

invoke to call on a subprogram, causing the subprogram to execute before control is returned to the statement following the call

iteration an individual pass through, or repetition of, the body of a loop

iteration counter a counter variable that is incremented with each iteration of a loop

iterator an operation that allows us to process—one at a time—all the components in an object

key a member of a class whose value is used to determine the logical and/or physical order of the items in a list

layout manager a method in the `Frame` class that automatically manages the placement of display elements within this particular style of window on the screen

length the number of items in a list; the length can vary over time

lifetime for a variable, constant, or object, the portion of an application's execution time during which it is assigned storage space in the computer's memory

linear relationship each element except the first has a unique predecessor, and each element except the last has a unique successor

linear time for an algorithm, when the big-O work expression can be expressed in terms of a constant times n, where n is the number of values in a data set

listing a copy of a source program, output by a compiler, containing messages to the programmer

literal value any constant value written in a program

local variable a variable declared within a block; it is not accessible outside of that block

local data data that is associated with a specific call to a method

logarithmic order for an algorithm, when the big-O work expression can be expressed in terms of the logarithm of n, where n is the number of values in a data set

logical order the order in which the programmer wants the statements in the program to be executed, which may differ from the physical order in which they appear

loop a method of structuring statements so that they are repeated while certain conditions are met

loop control variable (lcv) a variable whose value is used to determine whether the loop executes another iteration or exits

loop entry the point at which the flow of control first passes to a statement inside a loop

loop exit that point when the repetition of the loop body ends and control passes to the first statement following the loop

loop test the point at which the loop expression is evaluated and the decision is made either to begin a new iteration or skip to the statement immediately following the loop

machine language the language, made up of binary-coded instructions, that is used directly by the computer

mainframe a large computing system designed for high-volume processing or for use by many people at once

maintenance the modification of a program, after it has been completed, in order to meet changing requirements or to take care of any errors that show up

maintenance phase period during which maintenance occurs

mantissa with respect to floating-point representation of real numbers, the digits representing a number itself and not its exponent

member a field or method declaration within a class

memory unit internal data storage in a computer

metalanguage a language that is used to write the syntax rules for another language

method a subprogram that defines one aspect of the behavior of a class; a subprogram in Java

microcomputer see *personal computer*

mixed type expression an expression that contains operands of different data types; also called a mixed mode expression

modifiability the property of an encapsulated class definition that allows the implementation to be changed without having an effect on code that uses it (except in terms of speed or memory space)

modular programming see *top-down design*

modularity (in OOD) meaningful packaging of objects

module a self-contained collection of steps that solves a problem or subproblem; can contain both concrete and abstract steps

mutable an object whose state can be changed after it is created

named constant a location in memory, referenced by an identifier, where a data value that cannot be changed is stored

narrowing conversion a type conversion that may result in a loss of some information, as in converting a value of type `double` to type `float`

nested control structure a program structure consisting of one control statement (selection, iteration, or subprogram) embedded within another control statement

nested if an *if* statement that is nested within another *if* statement

nested loop a loop that is within another loop

new an operator that takes a class name and returns an object of the class type

object a collection of data values and associated operations

object (general sense) an entity or thing that is relevant in the context of a problem

object (Java) an instance of a class

object code a machine language version of a source code

object-oriented design a technique for developing software in which the solution is expressed in terms of objects—self-contained entities composed of data and operations on that data that interact by sending messages to one another

object program the machine-language version of a source program

object-based programming language a programming language that supports abstraction and encapsulation, but not inheritance

observer an operation that allows us to observe the state of an instance of an abstract data type without changing it

one-dimensional array a structured collection of components of the same type given a single name; each component is accessed by an index that indicates its position within the collection

operating system a set of programs that manages all of the computer's resources

ordinal data type a data type in which each value (except the first) has a unique predecessor and each value (except the last) has a unique successor

out-of-bounds array index an index value that is either less than 0 or greater than the array size minus 1

output transformation an operation that takes an instance of an abstract data type and converts it to a representation that can be output

overflow the condition that arises when the value of a calculation is too large to be represented

overloading the repeated use of a method name with a different signature

override to provide an instance method in a derived class that has the same form of heading as an instance method in its superclass; the method in the derived class redefines (overrides) the method in its superclass; we cannot override class methods

package a named collection of program building blocks or components in Java that can be imported by a class

parameter a variable declared in a method heading

parameter passing the transfer of data between the arguments and parameters in a method call

pass by address a parameter-passing mechanism in which the memory address of the argument is passed to the parameter; also called pass by reference (not used in Java)

pass by reference see *pass by address*

pass by value a parameter-passing mechanism in which a copy of an argument's value is passed to the parameter (used in Java)

password a unique series of letters assigned to a user (and known only by that user) by which that user identifies himself or herself to a computer during the logging-on procedure; a password system protects information stored in a computer from being tampered with or destroyed

path a combination of branches that might be traversed when a program or function is executed

path testing a testing technique whereby the tester tries to execute all possible paths in a program or function

PC see *personal computer*

peripheral device an input, output, or auxiliary storage device attached to a computer

personal computer (PC) a small computer system (usually intended to fit on a desktop) that is designed to be used primarily by a single person

polymorphic an operation that has multiple meanings depending on the class of object to which it is bound

polymorphism the ability to determine which of several operations with the same name is appropriate; a combination of static and dynamic binding

positional matching a method of matching arguments and parameters by their relative positions in the two lists; also called *relative* or *implicit* matching

postfix operator an operator that follows its operand(s)

precision a maximum number of significant digits

prefix operator an operator that precedes its operand(s)

priming read an initial reading of a set of data values before entry into an event-controlled loop in order to establish values for the variables

problem-solving phase the first set of steps in programming a computer: analyzing the problem; developing an algorithm; testing the algorithm for accuracy

procedural abstraction the separation of the logical properties of an action from its implementation

programming planning, scheduling, or performing a task or an event; see also *computer programming*

programming language a set of rules, symbols, and special words used to construct a program

pseudocode a mixture of English statements and Java-like control structures that can easily be translated into a programming language

public interface the members of a class that can be accessed outside of the class, together with the modes of access that are specified by other modifiers

range of values the interval within which values must fall, specified in terms of the largest and smallest allowable values

real number a number that has a whole and a fractional part and no imaginary part

recursion the situation in which a subprogram calls itself

recursive call a subprogram call in which the subprogram being called is the same as the one making the call

recursive case see *general case*

recursive definition a definition in which something is defined in terms of a smaller version of itself

registering the listener   adding the listener to an event source object's list of interested listeners

relational operators   operators that state that a relationship exists between two values; in Java, symbols that cause the computer to perform operations to verify whether or not the indicated relationship exists

representational error   arithmetic error caused when the precision of the true result of arithmetic operations is greater than the precision of the machine

reserved word   a word that has special meaning in a programming language; it cannot be used as an identifier

responsibility algorithms   the algorithms for the class methods in an object-oriented design; the phase in the design process where the algorithms are developed

return   the point at which the flow of control comes back from executing a method

reuse   the ability to import a class into any program without additional modification to either the class or the program; the ability to extend the definition of a class

right-justified   placed as far to the right as possible within a fixed number of character positions

robust   a descriptive term for a program that can recover from erroneous inputs and keep running

scalar data type   a data type in which the values are ordered and each value is atomic (indivisible)

scenarios (in OOD)   the phase in an object-oriented design in which responsibilities are assigned to the classes

scope of access (scope)   the region of program code where it is legal to reference (use) an identifier

scope rules   the rules that determine where in a program an identifier may be referenced, given the point where the identifier is declared and its specific access modifiers

secondary storage device   see *auxiliary storage device*

selection control structure   a form of program structure allowing the computer to select one among possible actions to perform based on given circumstances; also called a *branching control structure*

self-documenting code   a program containing meaningful identifiers as well as judiciously used clarifying comments

semantics   the set of rules that gives the meaning of instruction written in a programming language

sentinel   a special data value used in certain event-controlled loops as a signal that the loop should be exited

sequence   a structure in which statements are executed one after another

shadowing   the priority treatment accorded a local identifier in a block over a global identifier with the same spelling in any references that the block makes to that identifier

shallow copy   an operation that copies one class object to another without copying any pointed-to data

short-circuit (conditional) evaluation   evaluation of a logical expression in left-to-right order with evaluation stopping as soon as the final boolean value can be determined

side effect   any effect of one function on another that is not part of the explicitly defined interface between them

signature   the distinguishing features of a method heading; the combination of the method name with the number and type(s) of its parameters in their given order

significant digits   those digits from the first nonzero digit on the left to the last nonzero digit on the right (plus any 0 digits that are exact)

simulation   a problem solution that has been arrived at through the application of an algorithm designed to model the behavior of physical systems, materials, or processes

size (of an array)   the physical space reserved for an array

software   computer programs; the set of all programs available on a computer

software engineering   the application of traditional engineering methodologies and techniques to the development of software

software life cycle   the phases in the life of a large software project including requirements analysis, specification, design, implementation, testing, and maintenance

software piracy   the unauthorized copying of software for either personal use or use by others

sorted list   a list with predecessor and successor relationships determined by the content of the keys of the items in the list; there is a semantic relationship among the keys of the items in the list

sorting   arranging the components of a list into order (for instance, words into alphabetical order or numbers into ascending or descending order)

source program   a program written in a high-level programming language

stable sort   a sorting algorithm that preserves the order of duplicates

standardized   made uniform; most high-level languages are standardized, as official descriptions of them exist

state   the current values contained within an object

static binding   determining at compile time which form of a polymorphic method to call

string (general sense)   a sequence of characters, such as a word, name, or sentence, enclosed in double quotes

string (Java construct)   an object, an instance of the `String` class

structured data type   an organized collection of components; the organization determines the method used to access individual components

stub   a dummy method that assists in testing part of a program; it has the same function that would actually be called by the part of the program being tested, but is usually much simpler

style   the individual manner in which computer programmers translate algorithms into a programming language

subprogram   see *method*

supercomputer   the most powerful class of computers

switch expression   the expression whose value determines which *switch* label is selected; it must be an integer type other than long

syntax   the formal rules governing how valid instructions are written in a programming language

system software   a set of programs—including the compiler, the operating system, and the editor—that improves the efficiency and convenience of the computer's processing

tail recursion   a recursive algorithm in which no statements are executed after the return from the recursive call

team programming   the use of two or more programmers to design a program that would take one programmer too long to complete

termination condition   the condition that causes a loop to be exited

test driver   see *driver*

test plan   a document that specifies how a program is to be tested

test plan implementation   using the test cases specified in a test plan to verify that a program outputs the predicted results

testing checking a program's output by comparing it to hand-calculated results; running a program with data sets designed to discover any errors

text file a file in which each component is a character; each numeric digit is represented by its code in the collating sequence

throw the act of signaling that an exception has occurred; throwing an exception is said to abnormally terminate execution of a method

transformer an operation that builds a new value of an ADT, given one or more previous values of the type

traverse a list to access the components of a list one at a time from the beginning of the list to the end

two-dimensional array a collection of components, all of the same type, structured in two dimensions; each component is accessed by a pair of indices that represent the component's position within each dimension

type casting (type conversion) the explicit conversion of a value from one data type to another

type coercion an automatic conversion of a value of one type to a value of another type, called type conversion in Java

unary operator an operator that has just one operand

underflow the condition that arises when the value of a calculation is too small to be represented

unreachable a condition of an object wherein there is no way to refer to it

unstructured data type a collection consisting of components that are not organized with respect to one another

user name the name by which a computer recognizes the user, and which must be entered to log on to a machine

value-returning method a method that returns a single value to its caller and is invoked from within an expression

variable a location in memory, referenced by an identifier, that contains a data value that can be changed

virtual machine a program that makes one computer act like another

virus a computer program that replicates itself, often with the goal of spreading to other computers without authorization, possibly with the intent of doing harm

visible accessible; a term used in describing a scope of access

void method a method that is called as a separate statement; the method does not return a value

walk-through a verification method in which a *team* performs a manual simulation of the program or design

widening conversion a type conversion that does not result in a loss of information

word a group of 16, 32, or 64 bits; a group of bits processed by the arithmetic-logic unit in a single instruction

work a measure of the effort expended by the computer in performing a computation